W9-AQP-489

Kennikat Press
National University Publications
Series in American Studies

FREDERICK C. GIFFIN

SIX WHO PROTESTED

Radical Opposition

to the

First World War

National University Publications
KENNIKAT PRESS   //   1977
Port Washington, N. Y.   //   London

Manufactured in the United States of America

Published by
Kennikat Press Corp.
Port Washington, N. Y. / London

Library of Congress Cataloging in Publication Data

Giffin, Frederick C 1938–
    Six who protested.

    (Series in American studies) (National university publications)
    Bibliography: p.
    Includes index.
    1. European War, 1914–1918–United States.
2. Radicalism–United States. 3. United States–
History–1913–1921. I. Title.
D619.G58   322.4'4'0973   77-4724
ISBN 0-8046-9193-2

FOR MARTY, SCOTT, AND SHAWN
in the hope that, like
Henry David Thoreau, they
will never hesitate to
step to the music
which they hear

ACKNOWLEDGEMENTS

I have been richly assisted in the preparation of this volume. The research was made possible by grants from Arizona State University and the National Foundation for the Endowment of the Humanities. For reading the manuscript in part or in whole, and for suggestions, thanks are due to Professors Paul F. Boller, Robert J. Loewenberg, William W. Phillips, Ronald D. Smith, and—especially—James R. Kearney. I am also indebted to Grace Skinaway, Secretary to the Department of History at Arizona State University, whose skill as a typist was exceeded only by her unflagging encouragement and understanding.

CONTENTS

SIX WHO PROTESTED

INTRODUCTION

> War is the great uncivilizer of the age. . . . [It]
> sucks up the life-blood of a nation, saps the founda-
> tions of public virtue and private morality, and hangs
> a dark cloud over the future of humanity.
>
> —From a letter published in the *Indianapolis
> State Sentinel,* 16 August 1864.

In its relatively short history the United States has taken part in seven declared wars and has sent troops abroad, without the approval of Congress, over 165 times since 1798—an average of nearly one military intervention every year. Between 1775 and 1921, which of course includes the First World War, seventy-nine percent of the nation's total expenditures went for national defense—and "defense" can be a deceptive word.

Yet, while such statistics may lend credence to the allegation frequently voiced today that Americans have been a violent people, it is certainly the case that, throughout most of their history, they have not loved war. If—like the people of most other countries—Americans have immortalized war in song and story, so also have large numbers of them openly opposed their nation's military adventures. Indeed, some form of antiwar protest has accompanied nearly every conflict in which the United States has been involved.

During the Revolutionary War, when "Patriots" held the reins of power, many dissenting colonists rallied to the British standards or passively assisted the British cause. And these self-styled "Loyalists" paid a heavy price for their devotion to the Crown. They were not only intimidated, but their estates were confiscated and they were driven into exile—"to hell, Hull, or Halifax." According to the Patriots' definition, a Loyalist was "a thing whose head is in England, whose body is in America, and [whose] neck ought to be stretched."[1]

The War of 1812—or "Mr. Madison's War," as it was dubbed by critics—was one of the most unpopular conflicts in this country's history, and had it continued another year or so, it conceivably could have led to civil war. Ostensibly fought to protect American maritime interests, the war was actively opposed in New England, the nation's maritime section, where the damage to trade was most severe. The governor of Connecticut refused to furnish militia to the federal government, as did Governor Strong of Massachusetts, who even dispatched an emissary to the British to explore the possibility of arranging a separate treaty for New England. Moreover, as the course of the war worsened, antiwar sentiment spread to the South and the West, regions in which enthusiasm for the struggle had initially been keen. The War Department never succeeded in building up the regular army to half its authorized strength; and despite Henry Clay's boast that he could conquer Canada with Kentucky militia alone, that state provided only 400 recruits in 1812.

Ironically, this most unpopular of conflicts became highly popular after it had ended. The nationalistic surge which followed on its heels prompted many Americans to look back upon the War of 1812 as a fight for a free sea and a crusade in defense of national honor. Indeed, the struggle was scarcely over when orators were vying with one another in proclaiming its benefits. One South Carolinian even grandiloquently insisted that it had "given strength and splendor to the chain of the Union."[2] Conversely, it was considered necessary to depict those who had opposed the war as guilty of disloyalty, if not treason.

There also was resistance to the Mexican War of 1846—the first conflict in which United States forces occupied a foreign capital. Some critics of the struggle, like Senator Thomas Corwin of Ohio, denounced it as "a usurpation of authority," asserting that President Polk had violated that article of the Constitution which reserves to Congress the warmaking power.[3] Many branded the actions against Mexico a "slave owners' conspiracy" to obtain new soil for cotton plantations and new states for the South. Rather than support a war to aid the "slave power," Henry David Thoreau refused to pay his taxes and was jailed. His essay "Civil Disobedience" (1849) became the classic formulation of the view that it is the individual's duty to deny support or allegiance to a government that he believes to be wrong. Other outspoken critics of the war included the noted orator and reformer Wendell Phillips, minister and abolitionist Theodore Parker, Horace Greeley of the *New York Tribune,* and such political luminaries as John Quincy Adams and Daniel Webster.

Although—as in the War of 1812—hostility to the conflict with Mexico was strongest in New England, significant protest also emanated from the Midwest. Congressman Abraham Lincoln first attracted national attention by implying that the Polk administration had fabricated the incidents used to "justify" the war's declaration. The Illinois legislator was defeated for reelection.

Dissenters were numerous on both sides during the Civil War. In the North, the "Peace Democrats"—or "Copperheads," as they were labeled by the administration's supporters—claimed that President Lincoln and the Republicans had invalidated all attempts to settle differences with the South by sabotaging conciliatory measures. Their most brilliant and daring spokesman, Congressman Clement L. Vallandigham of Ohio, who declared repeatedly that a prolonged war could only mean the death of civil liberties, was arrested by Union troops in his hometown of Dayton on 1 May 1863 and was later escorted to the Southern lines near Murfreesboro, where he was turned over to the Confederates. In the wave of anti-Copperhead actions that followed his exile, armed troops broke up a rally on Vallandigham's behalf in Indianapolis, the *Chicago Times* was suppressed, and organized peace activity in the North was for the most part destroyed. Yet, in 1864 General George B. McClellan was nominated for president on a Democratic platform that condemned the war and the policy of the government in conducting it. McClellan repudiated the platform's call for a compromise peace but banked on Northern antiwar sentiment to elect him.

The major source of war-related mob violence in both the North and the South was opposition to conscription. At Industry, Texas, in December 1862, for example, several sizable bands of armed draftees attacked a Confederate officer and drove him away. And similar expressions of rebellion took place elsewhere, such as Randolph County, Alabama, where an armed mob, led by an active Peace Society, raided the county jail in an effort to free draft resisters imprisoned there.

In the Union, following Lincoln's order in 1862 that governors draft men if they could not fill their state militia quotas with volunteers, riots erupted in Wisconsin and Indiana, while there were threats of riots in Pennsylvania. The most notorious outbreak of violence, however, occurred in New York City several months after Congress enacted the first full-fledged national conscription act on 13 March 1863. Unfortunately, the law permitted a draftee to find a substitute or to pay three hundred dollars to sit out the war at home, thereby prompting many of New York City's Irish immigrants to regard the conscription act as a measure discriminating against them in favor of the rich. When the draft lottery went into effect in Manhattan on July 13, mobs consisting mainly of working-class Irishmen first looted and burned the draft offices, then turned their anger on free blacks whom they considered their major rivals for jobs. The rioters also menaced wealthy whites who had the misfortune to stumble on them.

It was four days before the disorders were halted—and only then after a detachment of Union troops arrived from Gettysburg. Total deaths in this worst instance of antiwar and racial violence in United States history may have been as high as 1200, while property damage was estimated at two million dollars. When conscription was resumed in New York City a month later, ten thousand soldiers were on hand to maintain order.

In 1898 United States troops participated in what Secretary of State John Hay termed a "splendid little war" to liberate Cuban insurrectionists from Spanish tyranny. Several months later the United States, now a colonial power, committed some 70,000 troops to extended and costly guerrilla warfare against nationalists fighting for the independence of the Philippine Islands. Although the Spanish-American War did not last long enough—and was too successful—for a substantial antiwar movement to develop, the campaigns against the Filipino patriots launched an anti-imperialist crusade that flourished for three years, drawing inspiration and sustenance from Americans who feared that colonial expansion would force the nation into the maelstrom of international power politics and destroy its democratic principles.

Prominent among the hundreds of politicians and private citizens who campaigned vigorously against American imperialism in the Philippines and elsewhere during the years 1898–1901 were ex-Presidents Benjamin Harrison and Grover Cleveland; Democratic presidential aspirant William Jennings Bryan; Speaker of the House Thomas B. Reed; reformers Carl Schurz, Henry Demarest Lloyd, and Jane Addams; writers William Dean Howells, Edwin Arlington Robinson, and Mark Twain (who called for a new United States flag "with the white stripes painted black, and the stars replaced by a skull and crossbones");[4] the editor of the *Nation,* E. L. Godkin; academic leaders David Starr Jordan of Stanford, William Graham Sumner of Yale, and William James of Harvard; steelmaster Andrew Carnegie; and labor leader Samuel Gompers. The sentiment common to these critics of United States expansionism was expressed forcibly in a statement released by the American Anti-Imperialist League on 18 October 1899:

> We earnestly condemn the policy of the present National Administration in the Philippines. It seeks to extinguish the spirit of 1776 in those islands. We deplore the sacrifice of our soldiers and sailors, whose bravery deserves admiration even in an unjust war. We denounce the slaughter of the Filipinos as a needless horror. We protest against the extension of American sovereignty by Spanish methods. . . .
> We hold, with Abraham Lincoln, that "no man is good enough to govern another man without that other's consent. . . . Our defense is in the spirit which prizes liberty as the heritage of all men in all lands."[5]

When the First World War broke out in the summer of 1914, a majority of Americans seemed determined to keep out of the conflict, viewing the carnage on the other side of the Atlantic as still further evidence of European society's corruption. Until 1917 the Woman's Peace Party, the American Union Against

Militarism, and other organizations laboring to insure the preservation of American neutrality enjoyed wide popularity and had administration backing. Antiwar sentiment reached a peak in November 1916, when President Woodrow Wilson was reelected on the slogan "He Kept Us Out of War!" and popular songs such as "I Didn't Raise My Boy to Be a Soldier" were sweeping the country.

Although a majority of Americans lined up behind the war effort following their country's intervention in April 1917, significant groups did not. Many Irish-Americans who supported Ireland's rebellion against Britain, for example, were distressed at the prospect of fighting on the side of England. Likewise, American Poles and Jews took a dim view of participation in an alliance that included Russia, while millions of immigrants from Germany and the Austro-Hungarian Empire were reluctant to take up arms against their kinsmen. Not surprisingly, the antiwar sentiment of these and other groups of Americans was particularly evident following the enactment of the Selective Service Act on 18 May 1917. It was in no sense a unique occasion when a crowd estimated at nearly ten thousand persons gathered late that summer in New Ulm, Minnesota, to discuss the bad aspects of the draft.

But the most determined opposition to the war came from the Socialist Party of America, an organization which was then a significant force in the nation's politics. Through the Socialist press and an incessant barrage of propaganda, the party and its leaders played an extremely important role as the focal point for all those who objected to the war and America's participation in it. During the early period of United States involvement, enough Americans agreed with the Socialist Party's stand that it did well at the polls. But, as the conflict ground on, the Socialists were hard hit by the policies of an administration whose mounting intolerance of dissent led it to prosecute actively more than two thousand people, many for simply speaking against the war— among them the Socialist Party's symbolic leader, Eugene V. Debs. More regrettable still, vigilantes pursued the administration's cause out of court. There were Fourth of July celebrations that included raids on Socialist Party headquarters; in Collinsville, Illinois, a young man of German birth who professed Socialist leanings but had no record of having opposed the war openly, was lynched by a drunken mob; and at Rutgers University—in what appears to have been the only campus riot prior to the Vietnam conflict—an antiwar Socialist student who refused to take part in a Liberty Loan rally was stripped, covered with molasses and feathers, and paraded through the streets of New Brunswick.

Another left-wing organization which suffered from both governmental repression and mob violence was the Industrial Workers of the World (I. W. W.). Ironically, this revolutionary labor union did not play a significant role in the antiwar activities which followed United States intervention. Although its members had long preached antimilitarism and antipatriotism as basic principles, after April 1917, the I. W. W. concentrated its energies on organizing miners, lumber workers, and harvest hands. Nonetheless, there was a widespread public belief that it meant to hinder the war effort at all costs, and the government responded accordingly. The union's strikes were broken, many of its alien members were deported, and the majority of its prominent officials and spokesmen were prosecuted and imprisoned. Indeed, by the end of 1918 the I. W. W. had been so effectively suppressed that it would remain crippled for years and, despite a re-emergence during the twenties, would never again approach even remotely its prewar vitality and organizational cohesiveness.

There were also more "respectable" citizens of the United States—individuals solidly entrenched within the mainstream of American politics—who actively opposed the war in at least its early stages. But they too found little tolerance for their views. The antiwar utterances of Senator Robert M. LaFollette, for example, were denounced on the floor of Congress as "pro-German, pretty nearly pro-Goth, and pro-Vandal,"[6] and the *Los Angeles Times* of 6 April 1917 ran a cartoon of a smiling Kaiser pinning an iron cross on the Wisconsin legislator.

National hysteria during the one year, seven months, and five days the United States was at war did not even exclude clergymen. As H. C. Peterson and Gilbert Fite point out in their book *Opponents of War, 1917–1918,* dissident ministers "were handled roughly, or even jailed." For example, in Newport, Kentucky, when the Reverend Herbert Bigelow attempted in late October 1917 to speak under the auspices of a loose organization of opponents of the war which went under the name of the People's Council of America for Democracy and the Terms of Peace, he was seized by an irate mob, bound, gagged, driven to a nearby forest, and lashed with a blacksnake whip. Similarly, in December 1917 an antiwar minister was one of two men overpowered by a mob in Audubon, Iowa, and dragged by means of nooses around their necks toward the public square. Both were released, but only after the minister's wife intervened on his behalf and the other man signed a check for a thousand-dollar Liberty bond.[7]

It should be noted that much of the abusive treatment accorded so many critics of the war could not be justified as a response to violent acts endangering national security. The only organized effort clearly aimed at overthrowing government authority occurred in Oklahoma in what is known as the Green Corn Rebellion. In early August 1917 about five hundred poorly educated tenant farmers and sharecroppers opposed to conscription planned to march on Washington, take over the governmental machinery, and declare the war terminated. En route the group intended to eat barbecued beef and green corn, destroy telegraph lines and railroad bridges to prevent military enlistments, and—hopefully—attract to their ranks thousands of supporters. These malcontents were easily rounded up by the authorities, however, and their leaders were sent to the federal penitentiary at Leavenworth, Kansas, to serve sentences of three to ten years.

It is estimated that during the course of the First World War approximately 170,000 "slackers" managed to evade the draft altogether by flight to Mexico or by obtaining false medical certificates or safe, exempt jobs. But these were not crusaders for peace. That role was far better filled by some four thousand conscientious objectors. The draft law and its enforcement were terribly confused, but in the end there were about twelve hundred objectors who accepted civilian substitutes such as farm labor; and ninety-nine took work with the Friends' Reconstruction Unit. Slightly over five hundred absolutists were court-martialed and sent to prison—the last of them gaining freedom only in 1933, long after objectors in foreign countries had been released.

There were seventeen conscientious objectors originally sentenced to death, but none were actually executed.

The Second World War was the only declared war in America's history to which there was practically no opposition. A handful of Trotskyists, anarchists, and I. W. W. members protested the conflict—and there were conscientious objectors on religious grounds—but most Americans supported the war as a struggle between the forces of light and darkness. As the veteran Socialist and pacifist leader Norman Thomas observed in 1943: "Opposition to active participation in this war, strong before Pearl Harbor, completely dissolved after the surprise attack by Japan and the Japanese and German declarations of war against the United States."[8]

There was likewise very little opposition to the "police action" in Korea. In fact, while there were approximately eight thousand conscientious objectors to that conflict, the only newsworthy incident of organized opposition was a rally of several thousand leftists in New York City on 2 August 1950. The overwhelming majority of Americans were convinced that the war was an international peace-keeping operation that could only be avoided by a dangerous yielding to the violence of international communism. Reminiscent of the World War I era, the support of some Americans for the government's objectives was of such intensity that when four workers in the Linden, New Jersey, plant of General Motors attempted to distribute antiwar leaflets among their fellow employees, they were beaten up, fired from their jobs, and expelled from the United Auto Workers.[9]

In sharp contrast to both World War II and the hostilities in Korea, the Vietnam conflict triggered an antiwar movement which came to be the largest in American history. The first murmurings of protest against American involvement were heard in the late 1950s. By the end of March 1968, when President Lyndon Johnson announced that he would not seek reelection, the protest had become an avalanche. The lonely battle, waged in 1964, by Senators Ernest Gruening and Wayne Morse—the only men in Congress to vote against the Gulf of Tonkin Resolution—had grown into a campaign fought by Majority Leader Mike Mansfield, Chairman of the Committee on Foreign Relations J. William Fulbright, and such other influential legislators of both the Republican and Democratic parties as Clifford Case, Frank Church, Vance Hartke, Robert F. Kennedy, and Thruston B. Morton.

Still more important as far as the war's continuance was concerned, Congressional opposition enjoyed increasingly vocal support from the electorate. Newspapers carried long lists of clergymen, lawyers, and writers opposed to the war; hardly a major university or city was without a draft resisters' league; on the nation's streets thousands—even tens and hundreds of thousands on occasion—held vigils, picketed induction centers and federal office buildings, and marched in peace parades; dozens of college campuses exploded in a spasm of violent protests over issues like ROTC, on-campus military recruiting, and classified war research; and the American role in Vietnam was denounced even by military professionals like Generals James M. Gavin, David M. Shoup, and William Wallace Ford. A Harris poll of November 1971 cited a sixty-five percent cross section of the population as believing the war to be morally wrong.

Although foreign policy always has been less susceptible to changes in public opinion than domestic policy, dissent against the Vietnam conflict accomplished what many of the protestors themselves deemed impossible. In 1971, after thirty thousand young people calling themselves the "Mayday Tribe" gathered in Washington, D. C., and dramatized their opposition to the "nightmare" in Vietnam by stalling traffic, blocking bridges, letting the air out of automobile tires, and rolling garbage cans in the streets, the government made strong moves toward ending the war. The Senate voted total American withdrawal within nine months if United States POWs were returned, and President Richard Nixon announced that he planned to visit Peking within a year in order to promote peace.

The movement against the war in Vietnam included much that was without historic parallel. Perhaps most notably, it was distinguished by its comprehensive nature, involving people from every part of America and all walks of life. Whether in San Francisco or New York City, small towns or major metropolitan centers, demonstrations commonly included housewives, businessmen, physicians, ministers, teachers, politicians, and even veterans in uniform. By way of contrast, most critics of the

War of 1812 were geographically centered in New England; the opponents of the Mexican War of 1846 derived largely from abolitionist and Free Soil movements; and the majority of those Americans who protested against World War I were from certain specific ethnic and radical groups.

Opposition to the American involvement in Vietnam was unique in several other respects as well. With the single exception of the losing effort of the South during the Civil War, in no previous conflict have its critics seen their case gain so increasing a degree of popular support. Moreover, in no previous American war were young people and students significantly in opposition; during earlier wars they were an important source of patriotic fervor. Nor is there any example of such widespread resistance on the part of the academic and literary communities. And finally, protest against the Vietnam conflict was exceptional for the extent to which it was tolerated. Serious federal involvement in the discouragement of dissent did not begin until the Director of the Selective Service System, General Lewis B. Hershey, wrote a directive to 4081 local draft boards on 26 October 1967 recommending the reclassification of some of the deferred protestors and their accelerated induction into the armed services as "delinquents."

Six Who Protested deals with but one small part of the long record of wartime resistance in the United States. It concerns the antiwar thought and activities of six representatives of the major branches of American radicalism during the early twentieth century who opposed their country's involvement in the First World War: the Socialists Eugene V. Debs, Morris Hillquit, Max Eastman, and John Reed, the anarchist Emma Goldman, and the syndicalist I. W. W. leader William D. Haywood. Emphasis is placed on what these noncomformists did, on why they did it, and on what happened to them as a result.

Since the individuals under consideration are treated in separate chapters, it is perhaps desirable at the outset to mention a number of their similarities and differences—both in background and as opponents of the war. All six were bitterly critical of capitalism and—except for Max Eastman, who saw the root causes of military conflict in man's bellicose and herd instincts—

all emphasized capitalism as a primary factor in the war's origin and spread. All shared a "selective" pacifism and limited opportunities to influence the formulation of national policy. While all six condemned the war and its "horrors," only Eastman and Reed had the opportunity to observe the conflict firsthand. Two of the radicals, Emma Goldman and Morris Hillquit, were of Jewish descent and had come to the United States from Russia; the remainder were native-born Americans of Protestant background. Finally, although none of the six engaged in acts of violence against the government, all but Hillquit—the only lawyer among them—suffered prosecution for their antiwar activities, and the three who lacked university educations were convicted: Eugene Debs spent two years and eight months in prison; Goldman was incarcerated for a year and eight months, after which she was deported; William Haywood was sentenced to twenty years' imprisonment, but jumped bail and fled to the Soviet Union. The trials of Eastman and Reed ended in hung juries.

Whether or not a study of radical opposition to the First World War will be judged of contemporary significance is open to conjecture. Doubtless, some readers more than others will find the work of value in increasing their awareness both of the controversial issues raised by dissent in wartime and, more generally, of America's ongoing conflict between individual rights and government imperatives. It is hoped, however, that all of the book's readers will share the author's conviction that an understanding of the past is especially relevant to any nation's search for identity, and that—in acquiring this understanding— defeated causes and minority viewpoints are as important as those programs that resulted in policies.

CHAPTER ONE

EUGENE V. DEBS

(1855–1926)

MISSIONARY OF AMERICAN SOCIALISM

You smug-faced crowds with kindling eye
Who cheer when soldier lads march by,
Sneak home and pray you'll never know
The hell where youth and laughter go.

—Siegfried Sassoon in *Debs and
the Poets,* 1920.

Few radicals have had a more profound impact on the people of
their generation than Eugene Victor Debs, the great moral force
of American Socialism. An ardent crusader with a burning hatred
of all forms of social injustice, he was perhaps the most controversial—yet popular and effective—Socialist figure ever to appear
in America. The acrimonious English dramatist and critic George
Bernard Shaw announced that "the only safe place for an honest
man like Debs" was the White House; Clarence Darrow, the
famous lawyer, considered him the kindliest, gentlest, most
generous man he had ever known; the British-American novelist,
critic, and biographer Frank Harris wrote of him as "the man
who had more of the spirit of Jesus in him than any man I have
ever met"; and on the occasion of his death in 1926 the *Nation*
asserted that he belonged "to the republic of the immortals
whose memory is a living inspiration to mankind." In sharp contrast, Justice Oliver Wendell Holmes dismissed Debs as a "noted
agitator"; the *Chicago Herald* described him as a "reckless, rant-
ing . . . lawbreaker"; the *New York Times* referred to him on one

occasion as "an enemy of the human race," and Theodore Roosevelt declared that Debs had "done as much to discredit the labor movement as the worst speculative financiers or most unscrupulous employers of labor and debauchers of legislatures" had done "to discredit honest capitalists and fair-dealing business men."[1]

There was little in the circumstances of Debs's early life to foretell the unique place he would occupy in the history of American radicalism. He was born in a plain wooden shack in Terre Haute, Indiana, in 1855. His parents, who had come to America from Colmar, Alsace, in 1849, were poor, hard-working people. Of ten children, only six reached adult age. Owing to financial hardship, schooling stopped for Eugene at fourteen, and he went to work in the shops of the Terre Haute and Indianapolis Railway, later becoming a locomotive fireman. In 1874 he quit his fireman's job and became a clerk in a wholesale grocery store. But his years with the railroad had captured his imagination. When a local of the Brotherhood of Locomotive Firemen was organized in Terre Haute in 1875, he took an active part, and a few years later became national secretary and treasurer of the union and editor of its magazine. Throughout the eighties he not only continued to work for the union, but also spent several years (1879–83) as city clerk of Terre Haute and served one term as a Democrat in the Indiana legislature.

An opponent of the craft-union philosophy, in 1893 Debs took part in the formation of the American Railway Union, which was open to all railworkers regardless of their particular jobs. With Debs as its president, in April 1894 the new union gained nationwide prominence in a successful strike against the Northern Pacific Railroad. Two months later, when employees of the Pullman Company at South Chicago went on strike, the American Railway Union agreed to aid them by refusing to move Pullman cars. Though Debs had initially opposed the action as inexpedient, once the decision was made he bent every effort to support the strike. And he paid dearly for his trouble. Concurrent with the arrival of federal troops sent by President Cleveland to maintain order and prevent interference with the delivery of the mail, the federal court in Chicago issued a sweeping injunction against the strikers and, in February 1895, Debs was sentenced to six months in the McHenry County jail at Woodstock, Illinois.

According to Debs's own word, he spent much of his time while imprisoned reading the works of Karl Marx and of the English Socialist Robert Blatchford, as a consequence of which he came to regard the Pullman episode as a practical lesson in the class struggle. In later years he encouraged the view that he had emerged from the Woodstock jail at the end of 1895 as a radical well on the way to Socialism. Yet, in 1896, Debs was in fact a Populist. He refused to contest Bryan's nomination and, indeed, supported the Great Commoner actively.

In 1897, the year that he announced his conversion to Socialism, Debs transformed what was left of the American Railway Union into a colonization group known as the Social Democracy of America. Three years later he and many others among the Social Democracy people joined the dissident wing of Daniel De Leon's Socialist Labor Party to create the Socialist Party of America, though the name was not adopted until 1901. As his party's candidate for president in 1900, 1904, 1908, and 1912, Debs gained national attention. In 1912 he polled six percent of the total presidential vote—an accomplishment never again equaled by a Socialist candidate.

It was under Debs's leadership that American Socialism enjoyed its greatest national popularity. Although he was at no time his party's intellectual leader—a role which demanded a more skilled theoretician—he was clearly its spiritual leader, its soul and its heart. The empathy with the downtrodden and exploited that other men only talked about, Debs seemed to feel genuinely. While he lacked the hard-headedness of the politician and often stood aside, not participating in party discussions or attending party conventions, he was unrivaled in his ability to communicate the urgency of the class struggle and the Socialist vision of a future society liberated from capitalism. A revolutionist in a profoundly moral sense (Socialist Kate Richards O'Hare described him to Samuel Castleton in a letter of 16 September 1945 as "our Carpenter of Nazareth"), like many other radicals he often mentioned God in his public addresses.

A man of extraordinary oratorical gifts, Debs was at his best on the platform, communicating with mass audiences. His diction was good and he refrained from the sectarian phraseology common to so many of his Socialist colleagues. The judgment of his contemporary Alexander Trachtenberg, that "Debs was the most eloquent speaker the American labor movement has produced,"[2] was supported by others who had an opportunity to hear him. According to the poet and playwright Max Ehrmann, whose admiration for Debs rarely distorted his judgment or subdued his critical acumen,

Whatever may be said of his philosophy, one thing is certain, that he has won a place in American history as one of its greatest orators; and in my opinion, there is not a man on the American platform to-day, who is his equal. His is a new and different kind of oratory. He resorts to no trick of rhetoric; no claptrap and stage effects, no empty pretense of deep emotion; but he stands frankly before his audiences and opens the doorways of his mind and heart that seem ever to be overflowing with terrible invective or the sweet waters of human kindness.[3]

For all his love of humanity, Eugene Debs was far from being the incarnation of Christ described by his most ardent supporters. A seer of visions? A dreamer of dreams? Most certainly. A "man whose gentleness and sweet, passionate anguish touched a chord of goodness in more Americans than probably any other figure in American life after Lincoln"?[4] Perhaps. But not a saint—unless saints are prone to all the ills that flesh is heir to. Like most idealists who get carried away by their hatred of injustice Debs suffered from an inflexible morality. His language, both of denunciation and of praise, was often extreme, and his social philosophy left no room for compromise. He was intellectually rigid, inconsistent, and prone to exaggeration. He was, in short, very human—a characteristic nowhere more evident than in the record of his campaign against war.

From almost the beginning of his career as a Socialist Debs was an outspoken opponent of war, holding that modern wars have invariably been due to economic competition and commercial rivalry among nations in their struggle for world power. In 1900, during his first presidential campaign, he presented himself as an ambassador of peace, informing the crowds who gather to hear him that greed motivated American intervention in the Philippines, and that a Socialist victory would hasten the day when war "shall curse this earth no more." Toward the end of his third presidential campaign, in October 1908, he told an audience of ten thousand in New York City: "With the end of industrial and commercial competition comes the end of war, and with the beginning of world-wide cooperation comes the inauguration of the reign of peace on earth and good will toward all men."[5]

For Debs war was "a survival of the black ages of slavery, superstition and ignorance." The workers, rather than letting the capitalists make cannon fodder of them, should "be aroused to graple [sic] with and overthrow" this hideous atavism. To do so would not only be a service to mankind, but would be in their own best interests, for in time of war workers become no more than slaves "hired by the ruling class to shoot down other slaves." "Without the workers, who are at the same time its misguided supporters and its mutilated and bleeding victims," Debs believed, war would disappear and become "a horrid nightmare of history." "The working class alone makes war possible and only the working class can put an end to war."[6]

When the First World War broke out in August 1914 and the great majority of European Socialists "betrayed the workers" and supported the belligerence of their respective governments, Debs was heartsick. In believing that his comrades across the Atlantic would prevent the war, or at least never support such a conflict should it come, he had sadly underestimated the strength of European nationalism. Together with other American Socialists he had mistakenly assumed that the power of the Socialist parties and their cohesion in the Second International constituted an insurmountable obstacle to a major war. Had not the International Socialist Congresses held at Stuttgart in 1907 and Copenhagen in 1910 clearly affirmed the notion of working class solidarity and adopted resolutions against war?

Debs and his American colleagues could condemn the "bourgeois" actions of their European counterparts, brand the war "imperialist," and then stand apart from it, because they were not subjected to the same historical pressures. The question that faced European Socialists in 1914 was whether or not they would side with their governments in an international crisis. The traditional antiwar position of Socialists in the United States was subjected to no such point-blank demand. They were thousands of miles from the fighting. And while they probably would have followed the example of their European comrades in resisting invasion, actual or threatened, no such alternative was ever presented to them. In 1917, when their own country entered the war, no threat of foreign invasion was involved. American participation in the conflict entailed the sending of an expeditionary force to Europe.

Less than a week after England declared war on Germany, ten thousand New York Socialists gathered in Union Square, branded the war a struggle for the extension of markets, and called for an embargo of munitions and food to all of Europe. The National Executive Committee of the American Socialist Party issued its first statement on the European war several days later. It declared the party's "opposition to this and all other wars, waged upon any pretext whatsoever" and urged "the national administration to prove the genuineness of its policy of peace by opening immediate negotiations for mediation and extending every effort to bring about the speedy termination of this disastrous conflict." In subsequent statements released in 1914–15, the American Socialist Party warned of a possible food shortage and called upon the government to seize food industries in order to "starve the war and feed America"; charged that capitalism "logically leads to war"; urged American workers to oppose war agitation; and attacked the "jingoistic press" and armaments manufacturers for seeking to stimulate war sentiment in the United States. In May 1915, following the sinking of the *Lusitania*, the party issued a manifesto declaring that "no disaster, however appalling, no crime, however revolting, justifies the slaughter of nations and the devastation of countries," and adopted a peace program calling for universal disarmament and urging the formula "no indemnities and no annexations."[7]

No American Socialist more wholeheartedly supported his party's opposition to the carnage taking place across the Atlantic than Debs. Temperamentally and intellectually unsuited for the tasks of practical leadership, he saw his role in explaining the war's causes and preparing the workers for the impending social revolution. Throughout the autumn of 1914 and the winter and spring of 1915 he campaigned tirelessly in behalf of peace and in opposition to the rising tide of militarism in the United States. In speeches delivered in cities across the Midwest, in Oklahoma and Texas, and on the West Coast the theme he presented over and over again was that the war was a contest between two groups of capitalists in which the proletariat of each side had nothing to win and much to lose. Far from being a war for freedom or human rights, the bloody conflict in Europe had resulted from economic competition among nations for markets for their surplus production.

There was little that was new in Debs's antiwar position. Yet, two factors enabled him to reach a larger audience than others who shared his views. The first was his great popularity among Socialists and trade unionists. The second was the vigorous manner in which he expressed himself. The strength of feeling which characterized his views on the war was evident not only in his impassioned orations but also in articles he wrote for the *American Socialist* and in his trenchant, biting editorials in the *National Rip-Saw.* Even Debs's most hostile critics were hard put to deny the intensity of conviction that flowed from his pen in such editorials as "The Easy Way to End War," published in the *National Rip-Saw* of August 1914:

LET THE CAPITALISTS DO THE FIGHTING!

Do that and there will never be another war. Not even a skirmish. They are not fools enough to go out and kill one another and the fools they hire for that purpose they hold in contempt.

The capitalists tell us it is patriotic to fight for your country and shed your blood for the flag. Very well! Let them set the example.

It is their country; they own it and therefore according to their logic it is their patriotic duty to fight and die for it and be brought home riddled with bullets and covered with flowers as shining examples of patriotic duty to the youth of the nation. . . .

. . . You never had a country to fight for and never will have as much as an inch of one as long as you are fool enough to make a target of your bodies for the profit and glory of your masters.

Let the capitalists do their own fighting and furnish their own corpses and there will never be another war on the face of the earth.

The task of the Socialists, Debs asserted, was to "do all in their power to open the eyes of the people to the causes of war and to the impending social revolution which is to sweep out of existence the ruling classes of all nations . . . and thus banish the curse of war from the face of the earth." He insisted that to work for peace in such a manner was in the best interests of "genuine patriotism," as opposed to the fraudulent species of that sentiment "surreptitiously inculcated in the minds of unsophisticated workers by their crafty and unscrupulous masters." Socialist patriotism, Debs proclaimed, must be a "wider patriotism—as wide as humanity." Whereas capitalists wrap themselves in their national flags to conceal the selfish desire for profits that drives them to wage war, the red flag must "never fly in any war, but the last war—war against war to obtain universal brotherhood and peace."[8]

Debs did not stop with exhorting his fellow Socialists and workingmen to strive for peace, but sought as well to enlist women and young people in the "war against war." Long an advocate of women's rights, he believed that if ever American women were given the vote, "a mighty advance will have been made toward ending the war." Indeed, he took the position that had women had the power to decide the issue of war in 1914 the slaughter raging in Europe would never have begun: "Woman is by nature opposed to the savagery of war and where her counsel is heard and heeded the lurid hell of horrors men call war is unknown." Now that war had come, the ladies were "needed as never before to mitigate its horrors and to restore the earth to peace and sanity." In similar fashion, he believed children to be "naturally sensitive to the cruelties and horrors of war," and urged them to "learn about the Socialist movement," for Socialism "teaches them that war is murder and a crime against humanity, and that it is their highest duty to dwell together in unity and peace, serve one another with all their hearts, and rejoice in the manifold blessings of a commonwealth of comrades." Quite explicitly, Socialism could teach the young what Christianity had not.[9]

Unlike many radicals a devout Christian (humorist Oscar Ameringer described him as "the only thorough-going Christian that I have met in the flesh in my three score years and ten"), Debs was bitterly regretful of Christianity's failure as a force against war. It was, he pointed out, the "Christian nations" that had gone to war in Europe. Churchmen, he complained in an editorial written at the end of 1914, "pray for peace, but at heart they are for war, for where their treasure is, there is their heart also."[10]

During 1915 and 1916 Debs was one of the handful of prominent men who tried to stop the United States's steady drift toward involvement in the war. By the beginning of 1916 the tide of American opinion had begun to run more and more against Germany, and advocates of "preparedness" such as Theodore Roosevelt and General Leonard Wood were urging that the United States should rapidly enlarge its military and naval forces in order to strengthen its defense against possible attack. Even President Woodrow Wilson became a convert to the movement. Though in a message of December 1914 he had disparaged the necessity for any increase in armaments, by November 1915 he had begun to change his stand. And by the beginning of 1916 he was publicly demanding "the greatest navy in the world."

Debs regarded "plutocratic 'preparedness' " as "nothing less than a monstrous conspiracy, a colossal crime of the ruling nabobs and their gilded gangsters against the common people." It was a plot to transform America into "a military oligarchy." As he saw it, the enemy that the workers needed to prepare against was a domestic and not a foreign one. "We have . . . no need to prepare against invasion," he wrote, "for the simple and sufficient reason that the country belongs not to us but to the capitalist class and we have nothing to be robbed of but our poverty and nothing to lose but our chains." His response to Theodore Roosevelt's assertion that preparedness "usually averts war . . . and always prevents disgrace in war" was that "any nation that today PREPARES for war INCITES war and slaughter." Roosevelt, he charged, belonged to that "bourgeois aggregation of patriots" who lack the courage to admit that they stand for war and instead hypocritically mask their belligerency behind such phrases as "peace with honor." Debs reacted to the former Rough Rider's advocacy of military training in the schools with the comment that he "would no more teach school children military training than teach them arson, robbery, or assassination."[11]

When President Wilson joined the preparedness crusade Debs

accused him of having "wheeled into line under the crack of
the lash of his Wall Street masters." The president, he asserted
in the *American Socialist* (12 February 1916), was just another
of those "stock-yard romanticists" and "pork-chop patriots"
who preach that preparedness and patriotism are synonymous
and that arming America "to its finger-tips and its eye-brows"
proves the American people to be "the loftiest of idealists."

While Debs was quick to attack Wilson and Roosevelt and
showed no hesitancy in denouncing "prominent capitalist preachers" infected by the "get ready for war fever," he adopted a
more tolerant attitude toward those American Socialists like
Upton Sinclair and Charles Edward Russell who, especially
after the torpedoing of the *Lusitania* in May 1915, were not
immune to the increasing clamor for war against Germany.
When Upton Sinclair circulated a statement supporting Wilson's
preparedness campaign, Debs abandoned invective in favor of
a gentle lesson in Socialist theory. The "workers have no
country to fight for," he wrote the well-known author. "It
belongs to the capitalists and the plutocrats. Let them worry
over its defense."[12] Similarly, he issued a statement in the *American Socialist* of 29 January 1916 asking that Charles Edward
Russell not be denounced or asked to leave the party for having
said in a speech in San Francisco that "we've got to have war
and . . . we've got to get ready the tools for war unless we wish
to see, instead of democracy, German autocracy dominate
the world for the next two or three hundred years." Though
Debs was in sharp disagreement with Russell, and had earlier said
so in a letter to the editor of the *New York Sun* (30 November
1915), he reminded the readers of the *American Socialist* that
Russell had long served the Socialist cause and that "but for
his utterance on the question of preparedness . . . would have
been chosen as the standard bearer of the party" in the approaching presidential campaign.

Debs's reaction to the *Lusitania* incident was in line with that
of the Socialist Party's National Executive Committee. According to a manifesto which the committee addressed to the American people in May 1915, the sinking of the *Lusitania* brought
home "the fiendish savagery of warfare and should inspire us
with stronger determination than ever to maintain peace and

civilization at any cost."[13] In a letter contributing to a symposium on the disaster in the *New Review* (June 1915), Debs wrote:

> Whom the Gods would destroy they first make mad. The criminal destruction of the Lusitania and the frenzied celebration of the great event in Berlin prove conclusively that Prussian militarism has gone stark mad. . . .
>
> Triumphant Prussian militarism would mean absolute reversion to feudal barbarism. It is the deadliest menace that confronts the world. . . . And yet I would not have the United States declare war on the Kaiser and his imperial government. Moral self-restraint at this crucial hour requires greater courage and is more potent for righteousness and peace than a declaration of war.
>
> . . . Let the monstrous massacre of the innocents carry its own tragic lesson and make its mute appeal to the moral sense of the world.

Germany was wrong. But the loss of some one hundred American lives was not sufficient cause for American workers to fight German workers.

In April 1916, following a speaking tour which took him to such places as Ann Arbor, Michigan, where he attacked the President's pleas for national unity and insisted that the workers had no interest in "capitalist war," Debs was nominated for Congress by the Socialist Party of Indiana. In accepting the nomination, Debs made it clear that he would run as a means of opposing Wilson's military preparations. His letter of acceptance included a scathing indictment of the war and re-emphasized Socialist opposition to the conflict. The tragedy in Europe, he wrote, "has transformed nation after nation . . . into hideous slaughter-houses where millions of our brothers have been turned into brutes and shot like dogs." Socialism was "diametrically opposed" to this "lurid scene of crime and horror." The Socialist Party "stands for . . . mutual interests and good will among men, for the prosperity and peace of all—for a free people and a happy world."[14]

Debs campaigned vigorously, covering the Fifth Congressional District of Indiana by auto, driving seventy-five to one hundred forty miles and delivering as many as eleven speeches a day. The major themes of his campaign—vigorously argued in the more than one million pieces of literature distributed for him—was that the two major parties could not be antiwar because they were procapitalist and propreparedness. Although his opposition to preparedness probably cost him several thousand votes, he was unyielding on this issue. When Daniel Hoan, the Socialist Mayor of Milwaukee, took part in a patriotic preparedness parade late that summer, Debs branded the action a "perversion of principle" and a "vote catching" insult to militant Socialists.[15]

Debs's candidacy was enthusiastically endorsed by a number of prominent Socialists—among them George R. Kirkpatrick (the Socialist Party's vice-presidential candidate in 1916), James Larkin of Ireland, Alexandra Kollontai of Russia, and H. Scott Bennett, a former member of the Australian Parliament. According to Bennett, who, like Kirkpatrick, spoke tirelessly on Debs's behalf throughout the entire district, no one had "more clearly defined his attitude toward war and preparedness than Debs."[16]

Bennett had in mind not only the war in Europe, but the Mexican crisis. In July Debs had briefly interrupted his campaign to protest the United States position regarding the Mexican revolution. Following American recognition of General Venustiano Carranza's *de facto* government in October of 1915, civil violence had continued. In January 1916 eighteen Americans holding passports of safe conduct issued by the *de facto* government had been taken from a train at Santa Ysabel and shot in cold blood by forces of the Mexican revolutionary Pancho Villa. Then, on March 9, Villa had raided the town of Columbus, New Mexico, killing seventeen more Americans. As a consequence, President Wilson had sent over 6000 troops under General John J. Pershing into Mexico to catch the raiders. Debs, following the lead of the Socialist Party's National Executive Committee, had blamed the crisis on "lies manufactured by the subsidized capitalist press" and had demanded an immediate end to the intervention. The whole affair, he had written in the *American Socialist* (22 July 1916), is backed by "Wall Street, which has over two billions of dollars invested in Mexico" and wants to force the peons "back into the mines and smelters to work for a miserable 15 cents a day." If war should result, if "the workingmen of the United States are called upon to murder the workingmen of Mexico," only "the powers that be" would benefit. To his relief, the crisis was resolved short of war.

Following his unsuccessful race for Congress, Debs embarked

on a speaking tour of the Eastern states, climaxing his efforts with a big antiwar rally at Cooper Union in New York City. Everywhere he went he was met by overflow crowds. "I have never seen such extraordinary Socialist meetings. . . . The largest auditoriums have been packed and jammed to the last foot of standing room and thousands turned away," he wrote at the close of the tour. "Anti-war, anti-militarism, anti-high cost of living, and anti-capitalism, imperialism or plutocracy is what appeals to the people and the more radical it is the better it suits and the more enthusiastic is the applause."[17]

During the course of his antiwar activities in 1915–17 Debs advanced two proposals on how to keep the United States from joining the conflict. Neither of them was original with him. The first (which had its origins in an earlier declaration of the Socialist Second International and which Debs never actually tried to implement) was for American workers to declare a nationwide general strike should Congress declare war. The second was a pet idea of Allan L. Benson, the Socialist Party's presidential candidate in 1916, and had been included in the party's 1916 platform. Debs urged a "constitutional amendment providing that no war shall be declared except by a vote of the people and that, . . . if war is declared they who voted for it shall be the first to go to the front. . . ." He believed that the people of the United States were against war and that the requirement of a national referendum "would put an end to war forever in this country."[18]

Although many of Debs's utterances betray pacifist notions, he did not reject violence under all circumstances. He believed that wars waged by the workers against their capitalist overlords were acceptable, even necessary, for the class that did not struggle for civil and industrial rights would remain forever enslaved. Hence he could argue in favor of "war against slavery and for emancipation" and proclaim that "when the law fails, and in fact, becomes the bulwark of crime and oppression, then an appeal to force is not only justified but becomes a patriotic . duty." In September and December of 1915, in response to accusations on the part of some of his militant Socialist colleagues that he harbored pacifist illusions, Debs published two articles that made his support for the "war of social revolution" unmistakably clear. "I have been asked if I was opposed to all war and if I would refuse to be a soldier and fight under any circumstances, he wrote in the *Appeal to Reason*.

No, I am not opposed to all war, nor am I opposed to fighting under all circumstances. . . . When I say I am opposed to war, I mean ruling class war. . . . It matters not to me whether this war be offensive or defensive, or what other lying excuse may be invented for it, I am opposed to it, and I would be shot for treason before I would enter such a war. . . .

. . . Capitalist conquest and capitalist plunder must be fought by the capitalists themselves so far as I am concerned, and upon that question there can be no compromise and no misunderstanding as to my position. . . .

. . . But while I have not a drop of blood to shed for the oppressors of the working class and the robbers of the poor, . . . I have a heart-full to shed for their victims when it shall be needed in the war for their liberation.

I am not a capitalist soldier; I am a proletarian revolutionist. I do not belong to the regular army of the plutocracy, but to the irregular army of the people. I refuse to obey any command to fight from the ruling class, but I will not wait to be commanded to fight for the working class.

I am opposed to every war but one; I am for that war with heart and soul, and that is the world-wide war of the social revolution. In that war I am prepared to fight in any way the ruling class may make necessary, even to the barricades.

There is where I stand and where I believe the Socialist party stands, or ought to stand, on the question of war.

His message in the *American Socialist* was the same. "It is our duty to enlist in our own war and fight our own battles. But first of all we shall have to organize, equip, train and drill our army. . . . " Then, "when the capitalists declare war on one another, it is . . . for us to declare war on them all . . . and fight every battle for the overthrow of the ruling class."[19]

Early in the spring of 1917, not long after the conclusion of his Eastern speaking tour, Debs's worst fears were realized. On April 6, in response to President Wilson's war message, Congress committed the United States to the struggle on the other side of the Atlantic, thereby abandoning more than a century of noninvolvement in European quarrels.

On the day following the declaration of war an emergency national convention of the American Socialist Party opened at the Planter's Hotel in St. Louis, Missouri, to announce opposition to the action. The majority report of the Committee on War and

Militarism was read by Morris Hillquit on the fifth day of the convention. A restatement of the classic Marxist analysis of war, it was supported by eighty percent of the nearly two hundred delegates present and was subsequently endorsed by a national referendum of the party's membership. The report proclaimed the party's "unalterable opposition" to the conflict, blamed America's entry on "predatory capitalists," and proposed a seven-point program of opposition:

1. Continuous, active, and public opposition to the war, through demonstrations, mass petitions, and all other means within our power.

2. Unyielding opposition to all proposed legislation for military or industrial conscription. Should such conscription be forced upon the people, we pledge ourselves to continuous efforts for the repeal of such laws and to the support of all mass movements in opposition to conscription. We pledge ourselves to oppose with all our strength any attempt to raise money for payment of war expense by taxing the necessaries of life or issuing bonds which will put the burden upon future generations. We demand that the capitalist class, which is responsible for the war, pay its cost. Let those who kindled the fire, furnish the fuel.

3. Vigorous resistance to all reactionary measures, such as censorship of press and mails, restriction of the rights of free speech, assemblage, and organization, or compulsory arbitration and limitation of the right to strike.

4. Consistent propaganda against military training and militaristic teaching in the public schools.

5. Extension of the campaign of education among the workers to organize them into strong, class-conscious, and closely unified political and industrial organizations, to enable them by concerted and harmonious mass action to shorten this war and to establish lasting peace.

6. Widespread educational propaganda to enlighten the masses as to the true relation between capitalism and war, and to rouse and organize them for action, not only against present war evils, but for the prevention of future wars and for the destruction of the causes of war.

7. To protect the masses of the American people from the pressing danger of starvation which the war in Europe has brought upon them, and which the entry of the United States has already accentuated, we demand—

(a) The restriction of food exports so long as the present shortage continues, the fixing of maximum prices and whatever measures may be necessary to prevent the food speculators from holding back the supplies now in their hands;

(b) The socialization and democratic management of the great industries concerned with the production, transportation, storage, and the marketing of food and other necessaries of life;

(c) The socialization and democratic management of all land and other natural resources now held out of use for monopolistic or speculative profit.

These measures are presented as means of protecting the workers against the evil results of the present war. The danger of recurrence of war will exist as long as the capitalist system of industry remains in existence. The end of the wars will come with the establishment of socialized industry and industrial democracy the world over. The Socialist Party calls upon all the workers to join in its struggle to reach this goal, and thus bring into the world a new society in which peace, fraternity, and human brotherhood will be the dominant ideals.[20]

On the surface the Socialist Party officially adopted a clear-cut antiwar position. But beneath the surface it was a house divided. Almost forty of the delegates at St. Louis objected to the majority report. More important, despite an increase in party membership of over thirteen thousand during the three months following the convention's adjournment, many of American Socialism's most prominent figures came out in support of President Wilson and the intervention. One such dissident, William English Walling, went so far as to complain in a letter to the editor of the *New York Times* (26 May 1917) that the antiwar proclamation drafted at St. Louis should have been labeled the "near-treason resolution"—a sentiment shared by a great many non-Socialists, including Woodrow Wilson.[21]

Although Debs refused to denounce men like Walling, he rejected as "base and cowardly" the charge that the majority report was treasonable and insisted that there are times "when to be 'treasonable' is to be true to revolutionary principles and to the cause of humanity." Yet, despite his conviction that the war belonged to the "vultures of Wall Street,"[22] he was unusually silent in the thirteen months following America's entry into the war. He had refused to attend the St. Louis convention, even when a special motorcade of the faithful was sent from St. Louis to persuade him to change his mind. He discontinued his lecture tours. He voiced no opposition to American subsidies to England and France, to the Liberty Loan, or to the conscription act. He did hold numerous meetings in Ohio, but they were mostly in the homes of friends, were poorly attended, and were largely ignored by the newspapers.

Unfortunately, the explanation for Debs's behavior in these

months is not clear. Probably he acted as he did for a variety of reasons. He was in poor health; he was discouraged; his wife, Kate, and his brother, Theodore, were urging restraint; and, perhaps most important, public sentiment was intensely hostile to critics of the war. Many of his colleagues were being arrested under the Espionage Act of June 1917, police raids on local Socialist Party headquarters were common, and it was difficult to find a receptive audience—or any audience at all. Debs's planned address in St. Peter, Minnesota, on July 3 was prohibited by the Minnesota Commission of Public Safety, which demanded a substitute who would "deliver simon pure patriotic Americanism on July Fourth." At any rate, for whatever reason, as one of his biographers has asserted, during the remainder of 1917 and the early part of the year which followed "Debs was certainly groping in the dark. He still believed in friendship among the world; . . . he still longed for peace; but he had no program. He was lost. . . . America had become a strange land, in which Eugene Debs was a bewildered and unnoticed vagabond." Even his attempts to cast ridicule on the belief that the war was being fought for "democracy" and his pleas for love between nations were strangely detached, almost passive.[23]

One of the few antiwar actions Debs took in this period was lending his name to the Peoples' Council of America for Democracy and the Terms of Peace, an organization formed by Morris Hillquit, Max Eastman, Scott Nearing, and a number of other administration critics in the early summer of 1917. A liberal and quasi-pacifist movement, which subsequently claimed to have strongly influenced the formulation and announcement of President Wilson's Fourteen Points, the Council attempted to bring together all those who felt that the United States had undertaken an imperialist venture and who were disturbed by the violations of civil liberties that were taking place at home. Although described by the *New York Times* as a "pro-German" and "pacifist" organization, it made no specific effort to oppose American participation in the war and did not attempt to develop a basic view of the war's social causes. Rather, it called upon the government to announce a series of democratic war aims, to repudiate any claims for punitive indemnities or forcible annexations of territory, and to defend the constitutional right of American citizens to freedom of speech and assembly. In any event, despite the fact that it was supported by organizations with a total membership of two million and was regarded as sufficiently influential for Samuel Gompers to set up a counter-agency—the American Alliance for Labor and Democracy—the Council was hardly committed to the type of vigorous opposition to war with which Debs had been identified prior to the American intervention.[24]

During the spring of 1918 a situation developed which brought Debs back into the fray. At that time many Socialists who had earlier opposed the war were beginning to feel a certain change of heart. Their assumption that the Allies and the Central Powers were equally in the wrong was seriously challenged by the harsh terms Germany imposed upon Bolshevik Russia in the Treaty of Brest-Litovsk. This German "iniquity" in attempting to crush the "first Socialist republic in the world," together with the seeming Allied repentance of past sins reflected in Lloyd George's speech of January 4 and President Wilson's more sweeping Fourteen Points, combined to create in Socialist circles a sentiment of greater friendliness to the cause of the Allies and a more profound hostility to the Central Powers. Hence, a strong movement sprang up for a special party convention to consider the possibility of modifying the uncompromising antiwar attitude of the St. Louis Proclamation.[25]

Although Debs lent his support to the movement for a special convention, when it was reported in the press that he had come to realize the error of his ways and was now a prowar advocate, he reacted with a vehemence which suggested that the passivity he had shown for the past thirteen months was at an end. Ordinarily, he wrote in May 1918, it had been a rule of his to ignore false charges and misstatements concerning him in capitalist publications. But "an exception appears in the report now being circulated . . . that I have changed my front and am now . . . appealing for the support of the administration in the prosecution of the war to the bitter end." This "false and vicious report," he insisted, is designed "for no other purpose than to create dissension in Socialist ranks and division and if possible disruption in the Socialist Party." Claiming that he had "not changed in the slightest" the views he had expressed in the *Appeal to Reason* of 11 September 1915 ("When I Shall Fight," as quoted earlier in this chapter), Debs stressed that there was nothing in the St. Louis Proclamation "to apologize for or retract." He explained that in calling for a special convention he was looking toward the adoption of a "more complete and comprehensive" restatement of the Socialist Party's opposition to the war, not a reversal of that opposition. The party, he concluded, should make its stand "so clear that there could be no doubt in regard to it either on the part of our enemies or our friends. . . . I have condemned the German majority Socialists and I am not going to imitate their perfidy, much as the capitalist press may abuse me for not doing so."[26]

Whether or not a special convention would have adopted the type of statement Debs desired is open to conjecture. The National Executive Committee of the party rejected the proposal for such a gathering on the ground that under the conditions then prevailing "a free exchange of opinion was impossible." The Committee expressed particular concern that "those adhering to the party's uncompromising anti-war stand would be placed in serious jeopardy if they attempted to express their views."[27]

As the weeks passed, Debs became more and more disturbed by the persecution of war protestors. Not only were many of his friends being imprisoned under the terms of the Espionage Act of June 1917 and the Sedition Act of May 1918, which together practically guaranteed that any opposition to the *status quo* could be interpreted as traitorous,* but an increasing number of people—politicians and prominent clergymen among them—were demanding that opponents of the war be silenced. President

---

*The Espionage Act made it a crime, punishable by a $10,000 fine and twenty years in jail, for anyone to "convey false reports or false statements with intent to interfere with the operation or success of the military or naval forces of the United States or to promote the success of its enemies . . . or attempt to cause insubordination, disloyalty, mutiny, or refusal of duty in the military or naval forces of the United States, or . . . willfully obstruct recruiting or enlistment service." (40 U. S. Stat. 230, 15 June 1917.) The Sedition Act (as the 16 May 1918 amendment to the Espionage Act was called) prohibited anyone, on pain of $10,000 fine and twenty years' imprisonment, to "utter, print, write or publish any disloyal, profane, scurrilous or abusive language about the form of government of the United States, or the Constitution of the United States, or the uniform of the Army or Navy of the United States, or any language intended to . . . encourage resistance to the United States or to promote the cause of its enemies." (40 U. S. Stat. 553–54, 6 May 1918).

Wilson condemned critics of the administration's war policy as "friends and partisans of the German Government"; Theodore Roosevelt expressed his "fathomless contempt" for those "who desire an inconclusive peace" and identified the American Socialist Party as "a traitor to the cause of liberty"; evangelist Billy Sunday expressed his conviction that "fellows who knock registration or conscription" ought to be lined "up against a wall" and shot "like any other traitor," and American Minister to Holland Henry Van Dyke asserted that dissidents should be hanged. So deep and unreasoning was the hatred and fear of the enemy by the late spring of 1918 that the Montana State Council, in an action that was not unusual for that time, ordered the public schools to cease using a textbook on ancient history that gave what was considered to be too favorable a treatment of the Teutonic tribes prior to the year 812 A.D.[28]

It was in this atmosphere that Debs, apparently feeling that he had no right to be free when others were in prison for saying what he believed, decided to abandon any appearance of restraint and assail the war with great vigor. It became his objective not only to arouse opposition to the war, but also to taunt the government authorities into placing him on trial. When Socialist leader James Oneal visited him in Terre Haute at the beginning of June 1918, Debs told his guest that he intended deliberately to violate the Espionage Act and take the consequences.[29]

When Debs failed to attract the government's attention in a series of antiwar speeches delivered throughout Indiana and Illinois during the first two weeks of June, he determined to take an even more outspoken stand in Canton, Ohio, arranging to address the final session of the Ohio State Socialist convention on June 16. Ohio had long been a radical stronghold and a number of Ohio Socialists had been arrested. Indeed, three prominent Socialist friends of Debs—Charles E. Ruthenberg, Alfred Wagenknecht, and Charles Baker—were then serving terms in Canton's Stark County Workhouse, located across the street from where Debs was scheduled to speak.

That Debs had every intention of playing into the hands of federal agents is clear from his comments to persons who spoke with him upon his arrival in Canton. Shortly after registering at the Courtland Hotel he was asked by Clyde R. Miller, a reporter for the *Cleveland Plain Dealer,* if he supported the St. Louis Proclamation. When he responded affirmatively and Miller queried whether he was going to say that in his speech at Nimisilla Park, the aging Socialist retorted, "I certainly am." Similarly, in replying to the advice of an Ohio Socialist named George Goebel that he be careful not to say anything that would provoke the authorities, Debs asserted: "I cannot be free while my comrades and fellow workers are jailed for warning the people about this war."[30]

Just before going to Nimisilla Park, Debs stopped by the Stark County Workhouse to visit the three Socialists imprisoned there for violating the Selective Service Act. This experience probably upset him, for he was noticeably grim later that afternoon when he mounted the plain wooden bandstand (conspicuous for the absence of an American flag) to deliver his address. Nor was his mood improved by the sight of agents of the Department of Justice and volunteers from the American Protective League* moving through the crowd of some 1200 persons checking draft cards—still less by the seizure of fifty-five young men who could not prove registration.

One of six individuals on the program, Debs was introduced by the chairwoman of the afternoon's proceedings, Mrs. Marguerite Prevy of Akron, as "the best loved and most hated of all men in the United States today." Surprisingly, though he spoke for two hours, he made but few references to war in general and none at all to the World War. Moreover, his remarks included little that he had not said many times before. The speech was primarily an appeal for unity within the party. He reaffirmed his support of the St. Louis Proclamation; praised the Industrial Workers of the World; referred to the Russian Bolsheviks as "comrades"; decried the persecution of his Socialist colleagues; denounced the evils of capitalism, and called upon "men and women who have the courage" to "do their duty":

---

*The American Protective League was a volunteer organization originated in Chicago in March 1917 for the purpose of reporting on disloyal or enemy activities, including infractions or evasions of the war code of the United States. Organized along military lines, it frequently investigated matters referred to it by the Department of Justice. By the end of 1918 the League had branches throughout the nation and claimed a membership in excess of 250,000.

Get into the Socialist Party and take your place in its ranks; help to inspire the weak and strengthen the faltering, and do your share to speed the coming of the brighter and better day for us all. . . .

. . . The world is daily changing before our eyes. The sun of capitalism is setting; the sun of Socialism is rising. It is our duty to build the new nation and the free republic. We need industrial and social builders. We Socialists are the builders of the beautiful world that is to be. We are all pledged to do our part. We are inviting—aye challenging you in the name of your own manhood and womanhood to join us and do your part.

In due time the hour will strike and this great cause triumphant—the greatest in history—will proclaim the emancipation of the working class and the brotherhood of all mankind.[31]

As Professor David Shannon has observed in his excellent history of the American Socialist Party, "when read today" Debs's speech "does not seem to be a strong criticism of America's role in World War I."[32] Even his limited references to war in general seem tame—especially when compared with the blistering language of some of the articles he wrote before America became belligerent. There is nowhere in the Canton speech language as provocative as that found in "Never Be a Soldier," published in the *Appeal to Reason* of 28 August 1915:

The working man who turns soldier today becomes the hired assassin of his capitalist master. He goes on the murderer's pay roll at fifty cents a day, under orders to kill anybody, anywhere, at any time. . . .

. . . This is the vile and abject thing we call a soldier. Lower than the slimy, dripping depths in which this craven creature crawls, neither man nor beast can ever sink in time or eternity. . . .

. . . War is the crimson carnival where the drunken devils are unchained and the snarling dogs are "sicked" upon one another by their brutal masters; where they shoot off one another's heads, rip open one another's bellies and receive their baptism of patriotic devotion to their masters' anointed moneybags in a thousand spurting geysers of their own blood and brains and guts.

Working men and women of America! Let us swear by all that is dear to us and all that is sacred to our cause, *never to become a soldier and never to go to war!*

In 1915, however, America had been at peace. When Debs spoke at Canton the nation was at war, and one could not say things that might be said under normal circumstances.

The reaction to the Canton address was immediate and strong.

E. S. Wertz, the United States Attorney for the Northern District of Ohio, who had appointed stenographers to record Debs's remarks, told a reporter for the *Cleveland Plain Dealer* that "No man in the United States is too big to be prosecuted under the Espionage Act," and promised that if he found that the controversial Socialist had made the remarks attributed to him, he would act at once "to have him prosecuted." The *Cleveland Press* saw no reason for Wertz to hesitate. In a bluntly worded editorial, it charged that in his Canton speech Debs had done "more to aid the Hun kaiser than all the pro-German Germans in America" and asserted that there were only two places where such "war obstructionists . . . rightly belong": Germany or the penitentiary.[33]

For some reason, perhaps because the government was reluctant to move against a man with so large and loyal a following, Debs was allowed to continue his crusade against the war unmolested for two more weeks. On a speaking tour of northern Indiana, he denounced war as a means of settling international disputes, condemned war profiteers, praised the Russian Revolution, challenged audiences to show him a Socialist who sympathized with the German government, and insisted that the capitalist press had distorted his comments at Nimisilla Park. At Mishawaka—as Debs recollected some years later—a crowd of "Babbitts and flag wavers" attempted unsuccessfully to prevent him from speaking, and the mayor of Elkhart, who had earlier pledged that Debs would not be permitted to appear there, left town just prior to his arrival. On each occasion court reporters were present to make stenographic records of his remarks.

From Indiana Debs proceeded eastward, stopping to assail the war in various towns in Ohio. On June 29 he arrived in Cleveland where he was arrested the next day as he stepped from an automobile to enter the Bohemian Garden and give a scheduled address to a gathering of three thousand Socialists. Following a night in jail, he was arraigned before Federal Judge D. C. Westenhaver and pleaded not guilty to the charge of having violated the amended Espionage Act. He was released on $10,000 bond with a trial date of July 30, subsequently postponed at his request until September 9.[34]

Although facing the possibility of twenty years' imprisonment,

Debs's commitment to the antiwar effort remained undiminished during the late summer of 1918. In mid-August he appeared before a conference of Socialist officials in Chicago, urging that there be no change in the party's attitude toward the war and asserting that, for his part, he could be called disloyal, branded a traitor, put in jail, or even sent to the gallows, but he would not betray his principles. With similar disregard for the approaching trial, he told a Labor Day audience in Akron, Ohio—and repeated the message to a crowd in Rochester, New York, three days later—that men like Theodore Roosevelt were as "Prussian" in their attitude as the Kaiser. On September 8 he appeared as the principal speaker at a Socialist convention in Detroit where he exhorted America's workers to "rise against industrial autocracy" and announced that even if he were "sent to prison by the powers of militarism," his message would not change. "I would much rather be a man in jail than a coward outside of it."[35]

The chief attorney for the defense in the Cleveland trial was Seymour Stedman, a capable individual who had earlier served as a Socialist in the Illinois legislature and would subsequently represent Max Eastman, John Reed, and several other defendants in the second *Masses* trial. He was assisted at Cleveland by three other Socialist lawyers: William A. Cunnea of Chicago, Joseph Sharts of Dayton, and a local practitioner named Morris Wolf. Clarence Darrow, whose commitment to freedom of speech overshadowed his support for the war effort, might have been Debs's attorney, but he was in Europe during the summer of 1918. He wrote the aging Socialist in a letter of July 20 that he was on his way to France and England and would be gone about two months, but that if he could ever be of any assistance he would give all the aid in his power. "I know," he concluded, "you always follow the right as you see and no one can do more. With love always Clarence."[36]

The trial began as scheduled on the morning of September 9, Judge D. C. Westenhaver presiding. The case for the prosecution was opened by Assistant District Attorney Francis B. Kavanagh with a statement of nearly an hour's length in which he identified the defendant as "the palpitating pulse of the sedition crusade." Stedman's reply centered around the argument that the amended Espionage Act violated the Constitution's guarantee of freedom of speech. In defending Debs's remarks at Canton he reminded the jury that Woodrow Wilson had written in his book *The New Freedom* that "wars are brought by the rulers and not by the people," and, noting the similarity between this sentiment and those expressed by his client, asked that the latter be judged by "his life" and "his deeds" as well as by his words.

The first witness for the prosecution was Clyde R. Miller, the reporter for the *Cleveland Plain Dealer* who had interviewed Debs shortly after the famous Socialist's arrival in Canton. Although he appeared to be personally sympathetic toward the defendant, his testimony was damaging. He related that Debs had reaffirmed to him his support of the St. Louis Proclamation and had expressed the hope that the idea of the Russian Bolsheviks would come to prevail in America.

Two other key witnesses called to testify on the government's behalf were Virgil Steiner and Edward R. Sterling, both of whom had taken stenographic records of the Canton address. The former, a young man of twenty, had been recruited by the Department of Justice; Sterling, a Canton attorney, had been hired as a stenographic reporter by the Socialist Party. Together, their reports formed the main evidence for the prosecution. Steiner's was the less complete of the two, and he admitted under cross examination that his knowledge of shorthand was meager and that Debs had spoken so rapidly that he had been unable to keep up with him. Sterling, however, had had twelve years' experience as a shorthand reporter, and Debs himself conceded that Sterling's version of what he had said at Canton was substantially accurate.

The third day of the trial saw the prosecution call upon a series of individuals, distinguished only by their presence in the audience at Canton, who stated that Debs had in fact given a speech at Nimisilla Park on June 16, and that his listeners included persons of draft age. Their testimony completed, counsel for the government informed Judge Westenhaver that the prosecution had presented its case.[37]

No witnesses were called for the defense. Stedman announced that his client would make his own plea to the jury following the opening of final arguments for the government by Assistant District Attorney Breitenstein. Although Alexander Trachtenberg

later claimed that this decision was an outgrowth of Debs's
role as a revolutionist, arguing that the aging radical would not
"permit his lawyers to use tricks known to the legal profession
to mitigate his status before capitalist law," a different explanation has been offered by David Karsner, Debs's authorized biographer. According to Karsner, Debs believed "it would be useless to make a defense when he held, in the first instance, that
the Espionage Act was a flagrant violation of the Federal Con-
sitution, and that the constitutionality of the act itself had
never been determined by the Supreme Court."[38]

Debs made his plea before a crowded but hushed courtroom.[39]
Apparently forgetting his 1895 conspiracy trial, he began by
stating that for the first time in his life he was appearing before
a jury in a court of law to answer an indictment for crime.
Though aware that he might be sent to prison for the rest of
his life, he admitted the truth of all that had been testified to
in the trial and asserted that to save himself from the penitentiary
he "would not retract a word" of all that he had uttered. But
he went on to maintain that there had been nothing in his
speech at Canton to warrant the charges on which he had been
indicted. On the contrary, his purpose was "to educate the
people to understand something about the social system" in
which they lived and "to prepare them to change this system by
peaceable and orderly means" into "a real democracy." While
it was true that he was opposed to the present form of government, Debs continued, "I have never advocated violence in any
form. . . . I have always made my appeal to the reason and to
the conscience of the people."

On the issue of war his comments were considerably more
provocative than those he had made at Canton:

I have been accused of having obstructed the war. I admit it. Gentlemen,
I abhor war. I would oppose the war if I stood alone. When I think of a
cold, glittering steel bayonet being plunged into the white, quivering flesh
of a human being, I recoil with horror. I have often wondered if I could
take the life of my fellow man, even to save my own.

Men talk about holy wars. There are none. Let me remind you that it
was Benjamin Franklin who said, "There never was a good war or a bad
peace."

. . . I have read some history. I know that it is ruling classes that make war upon one another, and not the people. In all the history of this world the people have never declared a war. Not one. I do not believe that really civilized nations would murder one another. I would refuse to kill a human being on my own account. Why should I at the command of anyone else, or at the command of any power on earth?

... Yes, I was opposed to the war. I am perfectly willing to be branded as a disloyalist, and if it is a crime under the American law, punishable by imprisonment, for being opposed to bloodshed, I am perfectly willing to be clothed in the stripes of a convict and to end my days in a prison cell.

... Much has been made of a statement that I declared that men were fit for something better than slavery and cannon fodder. I made the statement. I make no attempt to deny it. I meant exactly what I said. ... I can hear the shrieks of the soldiers of Europe in my dreams. I have imagination enough to see a battlefield. I can see it strewn with the legs of human beings, who but yesterday were in the flush and glory of their young manhood. I can see them at eventide, scattered about in remnants, their limbs torn from their bodies, their eyes gouged out. Yes, I see them, and I can hear them. I have looked above and beyond this frightful scene. I think of the mothers who are bowed in the shadow of their last great grief—whose hearts are breaking. And I say to myself, "I am going to do the little that lies in my power to wipe from this earth that terrible scourge of war."

Debs wanted to underscore his opposition to the war by reading a brief statement containing statistics on the extent to which profiteering had been carried on during the past several years, but Judge Westenhaver would not permit it. This was a considerable disappointment to the Socialist leader, for, aside from the bloodshed, he believed profiteering to be that aspect of the war most repellent to all men of conscience, regardless of their political affiliation.

To the accusation that his utterances had promoted the cause of the Imperial German Government, Debs responded that hatred for Prussian militarism had been ingrained in him since birth. How anyone could suspect that he was capable of sympathizing with "such a monstrous thing" was beyond him. Surely jurors could not consider it treasonable to point out that it was not the German people who had created militarism, but their rulers. The true villain, he insisted, was "kaiserism," an abomination that he despised with every drop of blood in his veins—and one which unfortunately was not limited to Germany. Kaiserism, together with the militarism which it spawned, raised its head everywhere there was exploitation, including the United States.

In concluding his two-hour plea, Debs informed the jury that, so far as he was concerned, their verdict did not matter for he was "the smallest part of the trial." But the verdict should matter a great deal to them. American institutions were on trial, he proclaimed, and on their future hung the welfare of the whole people.

By the time Debs had finished his remarks, any doubt about the trial's outcome should have been dispelled. He had offered no argument upon the evidence; he had refused to recant or to take back anything he had said at Canton; he had admitted obstructing the war; he had even declined to ask the jury not to convict him.

Judge Westenhaver gave his final charge to the jurors on the morning of September 12, instructing them on the provisions of the amended Espionage Act and pointing out that if it were found that the defendant, in his Canton speech, had had no criminal intent to obstruct the government's war effort, it was their duty to acquit him. He noted, however, that it was not necessary to prove that the defendant's remarks had actually caused insubordination, incited mutiny, and promoted the cause of the enemy. It was sufficient if the jurors believed that Debs had specifically intended to do these things. Westenhaver also told them they must disregard the accused's assertion that the Espionage Act was invalid because it violated the First Amendment to the Constitution. That, he said, was a matter for the courts to decide.[40]

Following six hours' deliberation, the jury found Debs guilty as charged on three separate counts: attempting to incite insubordination, disloyalty, mutiny, and refusal of duty in the military and naval forces; obstructing and attempting to obstruct the recruiting and enlistment service; and using language intended to incite, provoke, and encourage resistance to the United States and to promote the cause of the enemy. Saturday morning, September 14, was fixed as the time for passing sentence. Debs spent the intervening day at the home of a friend in Akron, Ohio, where he was visited by his lawyers and persuaded to take advantage of the opportunity that would be given him to address the court before sentencing.

The opening paragraph of Deb's final statement to the court

has probably been quoted more often than anything else he ever said or wrote: "Your Honor, years ago I recognized my kinship with all living beings, and I made up my mind that I was not one bit better than the meanest on earth. I said then, and I say now, that while there is a lower class, I am in it, while there is a criminal element I am of it, and while there is a soul in prison, I am not free." For the rest, Debs branded the Espionage Act as "despotic"; reiterated his commitment to change the existing social system by peaceable and orderly means; spoke movingly of the oppression of the workers and of his faith in Socialism; asserted that he had no fault to find with the court or the trial; and said that he would neither ask for mercy nor plead for immunity.[41]

Judge Westenhaver admitted his admiration for Debs's sincerity and courage, but expressed amazement at the latter's "remarkable self-delusion and self-deception" in believing that he was serving the cause of humanity. Mr. Debs's principles, Westenhaver insisted, were "anarchy pure and simple," and anyone who had sought, as Debs had, to "strike the sword from the hand of this nation" while she was engaged in bitter struggle against a foreign power was an enemy. Overruling a motion for a new trial, introduced by Stedman on the grounds of a faulty indictment and the introduction of improper evidence by the prosecution, Westenhaver sentenced Debs to serve ten years in the West Virginia State Penitentiary at Moundsville on each of the three counts upon which he had been found guilty, the sentences to run concurrently.[42]

Debs's behavior throughout the proceedings in Cleveland, especially the dignity with which he accepted the verdict, inspired a good deal of favorable commentary in the press. The opinion of the *New York Times* that he deserved "whatever of respect is due to the man who sticks to what he says and endures the consequences of his words without protest" was widely shared. The defendant's lead in refusing to find fault with the court was not, however, followed by many of his radical friends, whose reaction was typified by Rose Pastor Stokes and Max Eastman, both of whom had witnessed the trial. The jury, Stokes complained, was comprised of "old men" whose eyes were "blinded by securities" and whose ears were "stuffed with stocks and bonds," and she referred to Judge Westenhaver as "a man who rocked back and forth in his chair and only needed some knitting in his hands to complete the picture." Eastman repeated Stokes's characterization in a caustically written article for the *Liberator,* the magazine which had been founded in March 1918 as a successor to the *Masses.* [43]

In an effort to test the constitutionality of those sections of the Espionage Act under which the indictment had been returned, the case was appealed to the United States Supreme Court. Meanwhile, Debs was released on $10,000 bail with the stipulation that he refrain from speaking against the war and confine his movements to the northern district of Ohio and to cities close to Terre Haute.

Despite the prompting of his party that he make a nation-wide speaking tour on behalf of other victims of the Espionage Act, Debs observed the geographic restrictions imposed upon him as a condition of his bail. But he declined to discontinue his attacks on the war. In an appearance in Toledo, Ohio, at the end of December he told a large crowd, including policemen and federal agents, that, though he was "on dangerous ground" in saying so, wars are declared by the ruling classes, never the people. At greater risk, he added that according to those in power, "When men under command go out and slaughter thousands of other men whom they do not know and who have never injured them, this is not murder—it is patriotism." In subsequent addresses he asserted that the Espionage Act was un-American, that the deportation of alien dissenters was unconstitutional, and that "common people" gained nothing from war. [44]

The Supreme Court upheld Debs's conviction in a unanimous decision rendered on 10 March 1919, four months after the armistice and just one week after handing down its decision in *Schenck* v. *United States.** The Debs appeal had been made on three counts: that the sections of the Espionage Act which lim-

---

*The decision in the Schenck case was regarded at the time as the high-water mark of liberalism in freedom of speech. Speaking for a unanimous court, Justice Holmes had formulated the "clear and present danger" test as a canon of interpretation of the First Amendment. The test was as follows: "The question in every case is whether the words are used in such circumstances and are of such a nature as to create a clear and present danger that they will bring about the substantive evils that Congress has a right to prevent." (*Schenck* v. *United States,* 249 U. S. 47 [1919].)

ited speech were in violation of the First Amendment, that the indictment was not sufficient in form, and that the admission in evidence of the St. Louis Proclamation and of the record of conviction of five other antiwar Socialists was improper. While the Supreme Court did not pass directly upon the constitutionality of the Espionage Act, it held that the act was not an abridgment of the constitutional right of free speech. The Court's opinion was written by Justice Oliver Wendell Holmes, who stated that Debs had been guilty of a willful attempt to obstruct recruiting and that the jury at Cleveland had been properly instructed.[45]

The reaction to Holmes's opinion—from radicals and non-radicals alike—was sufficiently hostile to cause the celebrated jurist to complain to his friend Sir Frederick Pollock in a letter of 5 April 1919 that he was receiving "stupid letters of protest" from "fools, knaves, and ignorant persons" who mistakenly believed that Debs had been convicted because he was a dangerous agitator and that the charge of obstructing the draft was a pretense. Nor was the expression of such opinions limited to Holmes's mail. Ernst Freund, writing in the *New Republic,* charged that there had been no evidence introduced against Debs "to show actual obstruction or an attempt to interfere with any processes of recruiting" and asserted that to brand a man like Debs a felon was to "dignify the term felony, . . . and every thief and robber will be justified in feeling that some of the stigma has been taken from his crime and punishment." With similar indignation, Amos Pinchot pointed out in the *Appeal to Reason* that "if the decision in the Debs' case had been the law in England during the Boer War, David Lloyd George would about now be getting out of jail." Even Debs, whose deportment at Cleveland had so impressed the *New York Times,* denounced the outcome of his appeal. "The decision is perfectly consistent with the character of the Supreme Court as a ruling class tribunal," he proclaimed. "The Supreme Court to the contrary notwithstanding, the Espionage Law is perfectly infamous and a disgrace as well to the capitalist despotism at whose behest it was enacted."[46]

Opposition to Debs's conviction was underscored not only by the belief of many radicals that it was the product of what Morris Hillquit termed a "police court philosophy," but also by the fact that he had been sentenced at a time when Germany's defeat appeared certain. Moreover, many who disagreed with Debs's views and could in no way be described as radicals were appalled by the contrast between Debs's treatment and that of prominent dissenters in England, most notably philosopher Bertrand Russell. The latter, a man twenty-five years the American Socialist's junior, had been found guilty of a misdemeanor and sentenced to only six months' imprisonment for remarks widely believed to be far more damaging to the war's prosecution than those uttered by Debs.[47]

That opposition to the disposition of the case was not confined to Socialist circles is apparent from the reaction of Forrest F Black, a legal scholar who, writing six years after Debs's death, labeled the affair "A Judicial Milepost on the Road to Absolutism" and was convinced, together with Professor Zechariah Chafee, Jr., of Harvard Law School, that Debs's guilt had not been proven:

> Had our governmental officials forgotten that Edmund Burke, . . . Pitt and Fox and Lord Camden had opposed the Revolutionary War and that under the *Debs* decision, they would have been sent to prison? Did they know that John Bright denounced the Crimean War while that war was being fought and that Lloyd George impeached England's motives in the Boer War after England was in it? . . . Let it never be forgotten that Lincoln and Clay and Webster and Sumner opposed the Mexican War while that war was in progress, and boldly discussed the issues and criticized the policies of the Polk administration.
>
> . . . How many patriots who favored the incarceration of Eugene Debs knew that General George B. McClellan was nominated for President in 1864 on a Democratic platform that condemned the Civil War and the policy of the government in conducting it—and this at the very height of our fratricidal strife?

The opinions of Black and other critics aside, the government's wisdom in making Debs a martyr in the eyes of his many admirers is open to question. Yet, as one careful student of civil liberties in wartime has pointed out, "except for the fact that the lower court had permitted to be introduced in evidence so much extraneous matter, . . . the Supreme Court's decision should have been expected. Debs had invited conviction by addressing the jury himself and admitting that he abhorred war and had obstructed the war."[48]

During the month following the Supreme Court's decision, Debs waited at his home in Terre Haute for the order to report to the authorities in Cleveland for delivery to prison. The order came on 12 April 1919, and he was sent to the state penitentiary at Moundsville, West Virginia, on the following day. Two months later he was transferred to the federal penitentiary at Atlanta, Georgia.

The imprisonment of the sixty-three-year-old Socialist leader prompted a flurry of tributes from persons who felt that he had been treated unjustly and, like Russian-born anarchist Alexander Berkman, regarded him as "the Grand Old Man of the New Day." Perhaps the most moving of tributes paid him was from Helen Keller, at that time an active radical. That Americans were within their constitutional rights as citizens to agitate against the war was to her axiomatic, and she regarded the suppression of speech and of the press which resulted from the Espionage Act as nothing less than "Kaiserism." At the end of 1917 she had written anarchist Emma Goldman, who had been sentenced to prison under the Espionage Act for her antiwar writings and speeches, that the latter's "work must go on, even though all earthly powers combine against it. How can there be democracy unless people think and speak their minds freely—unless the minority is treated with tolerance and justice?" Miss Keller's words to Debs nearly sixteen months later were in a similar vein, though more emotional. "I write because I want you to know that I should be proud if the Supreme Court convicted me of abhorring war, and doing all in my power to oppose it," she informed him.

You dear comrade! I have long loved you because you are an apostle of brotherhood and freedom. For years I have thought of you as a dauntless explorer going toward the dawn and, like a humble adventurer, I have followed in the trail of your footsteps. From time to time the greetings that have come back to me from you have made me very happy, and now I reach out my hand and clasp yours through prison bars.[49]

Debs had no intention of allowing his status as a prisoner to silence him. On the day he was taken to Moundsville Penitentiary he told his friend David Karsner, "I enter the prison doors a flaming revolutionist—my head erect, my spirit untamed and my soul unconquerable." His words proved more than empty histrionics. He carried on his campaign against war and militarism from his cell. "My attitude has not changed one whit since I came to prison," he announced in a statement released in mid-October 1919. "I would not take back a single word; I would not retract a single sentence. I will make no promises of any kind or nature to obtain my freedom. It would not be freedom if obtained by any retraction, promises or apostasy. To me that would be the worst slavery." A year later he repeated the same message to Norman Hapgood, who visited him in Atlanta and subsequently reported their conversation in the *Appeal to Reason,* including Debs's assertion that he believed in free speech in war as well as in peace. Even more pointed was the statement which he issued through his attorney on 1 February 1921 in reaction to President Wilson's refusal on the previous day to commute his sentence as urged by Attorney General A. Mitchell Palmer. Dismissing Wilson as "an exile from the hearts of his people," he commented on the issue of national armament: "I would sink the navy to the bottom of the sea, disband the army and raise my naked arms to the sky. Then no civilized nation would dare attack us. That is the example I would hold up to the world. . . . I have looked into the muzzles of loaded guns, but I've never carried a weapon in my life. I am armed by being armless."[50]

Debs's greatest opportunity while in prison to press his attack on war and militarism came in 1920 when he was nominated as his party's candidate for president on a platform which, among other things, criticized the Democratic administration as responsible for America's entry into the World War, demanded the repeal of the Espionage Act, and called for a pardon for all those imprisoned under the act. Though prevented by his imprisonment from making public appearances, he was allowed to issue a number of statements in which he reiterated his opposition to war and maintained that there was little difference between the Democratic and Republican parties. The tone of his campaign is suggested in the following passage from a statement he issued on 14 May 1920:

I am a traitor, no doubt, in the eyes of Attorney General Palmer and the Department of Justice, and perhaps some of the American people, but the words "Thou shalt not kill" mean to me just what they say. I would not kill in defense of my own life, and certainly would not hire someone else to. Seventy per cent of the drafted men [in the First World War] applied for exemption. They were forced to fight—forced to go out and kill—and why? As for the German Socialists, I condemn them just as strongly as I do capitalists when they surrendered their principles and joined the movement to crush the world. Principles mean something to me. I am against war, and I would go to the gallows without the slightest qualm of fear, preaching my opposition to war.[51]

When election day rolled around, Republican candidate Warren G. Harding won one of the most sweeping victories in the history of American politics—a seven million popular majority and an electoral vote of 404 out of 537. Yet Debs did quite well, polling 919,799 votes, or over 3.4 percent of the total.

Not surprisingly, there was considerable sentiment for Debs's release from prison—much of it from the people who had taken strong exception to his views on the World War. Upton Sinclair, for example, wrote in the *Appeal to Reason* that, although he had disagreed with Debs's attitude toward the war, he had never sanctioned sending him to jail. "I said then, and I say now, that his arrest was a blunder, and his trial a worse one, and his imprisonment is a disgrace to our government." In similar fashion, John Spargo, whose objections to the St. Louis Proclamation had led him to leave the Socialist Party, asserted in the *Independent* that he saw "no justification for the exceptionally heavy prison sentence imposed upon Debs" and pointed out that not even Nicholas II of Russia or Kaiser Wilhelm II had kept people in prison whose only offense was the expression of antiwar views. Others, like George D. Herron, founder of the Socialist periodical *Christian Society,* appealed directly to President Wilson. "A more loyal and Christly man does not inhabit this needy and tormented planet," he wrote the President in late September 1919. "You will do America a service, you will do your own heart and soul a service, if you will immediately sign an order for the release of this good man from prison."

Wilson was unmoved by the appeals on Debs's behalf. When Attorney General Palmer recommended to him on 20 January 1921 that Debs's sentence to be commuted to end on Lincoln's birthday, the President responded with a curt denial. "I will never consent to the pardon of this man," he subsequently informed his private secretary, Joseph P. Tumulty. "Before the war he had a perfect right to exercise his freedom of speech and to express his own opinion, but once the Congress of the United States declared war, silence on his part would have been the proper course to pursue. . . . This man was a traitor to his country and will never be pardoned during my administration."[52]

Fortunately for Debs, whose confinement was having an ill effect on his health, President Harding proved less intractable. Debs was released by presidential order on Christmas Day, 1921, after having served thirty-two months of his ten-year sentence. He was not pardoned, however, and consequently his citizenship was not restored. Nor was his release popular in all quarters. There were many Americans who strongly condemned the commutation of his sentence, supporting the judgment of the editors of the Richmond (Virginia) *Times-Dispatch* that it was "a slap in the face for the mothers whose sons lie in the sacred soil of France and for every soldier who followed the nation's colors in the World War."[53]

Immediately after his release from the federal penitentiary at Atlanta, Debs went to Washington, D. C., to confer with President Harding and Attorney General Harry M. Daugherty. What transpired at their meeting is unknown, but Debs emerged from it as outspoken and determined in his views as ever. On December 27, just before boarding a train at Washington's Union Square which would take him to his home in Terre Haute, he told several hundred persons who had come to see him off: "With every drop of blood in my veins, I am opposed to war."[54]

In the years which followed, Debs's resolve remained unshaken, despite health problems which caused him to spend several months in the Lindlahr Sanitarium at Elmhurst, near Chicago. He never recanted a word he had uttered in condemnation of America's participation in the World War. On the contrary, his attack on his country's role in that conflict—and, indeed, on war in general—continued. "I opposed the war. I still oppose war," he announced in a 1922 speech in Chicago. "I said then, I say now, that I would not go to war at the command of any capitalist country on the face of this earth." On 9 July 1923, not long after accepting the chairmanship of the Socialist

Party's National Executive Committee, he sent a message to
the membership of the International No More War Demonstra-
tion (an organization formed to agitate for the abolition of
America's military forces and for amending the Constitution to
deprive Congress of the power either to declare or finance war),
asserting that the time had come for "our so-called civilization
to put an end to the unspeakable savagery of war." Three months
later, he wrote in a radical weekly published in Omaha, Nebraska,
that the American soldiers who had lost their lives in the World
War had died in order to produce thirty thousand new million-
aires in the United States. At the end of October 1923, he informed a crowd of two thousand in New York City that he had
stood in the World War "where Woodrow Wilson stood within
five weeks of the entry of America into the war. . . . He was
elected President for keeping us out of war; I was sentenced to
ten years for trying to do the same thing. . . . I had rather a
thousand times be a man without a country than a man without
character." In May 1925, speaking before an audience of fifteen
thousand in New York's Madison Square Garden, he announced
the wish that "the workers of this country were patriotic enough
to refuse to fight in any war."[55]

Debs's last words on war were expressed to Arthur Robinson,
who interviewed him at the end of September 1926, just a few
weeks before his death. They reveal the remarkable blend of
realism and naiveté so characteristic of his views on the subject:

The League of Nations, as at present constituted, representing, as it
does, rival nations, cannot and will not prevent war. The Hague Peace
Tribunal has existed and held regular sessions over a period of many years,
but all its efforts to harmonize the relations of member nations and prevent war proved vain and futile.

Nations that deem it necessary to arm themselves against each other,
especially those claiming to be Christian nations, will never put an end
to war or bring peace to the world while they maintain that spirit and
attitude.

But war will one day be outlawed and banished forever from the face
of the earth as a hideous and monstrous abomination. That time will come
only when modern nations are really civilized and treat war as race murder,
and when exploitation ceases at home and competition abroad for control
of the market comes to an end.

If the United States had sufficient faith in its own moral rectitude to disarm completely on its own individual account and hold up its naked hands before the world it would compel general disarmament by the force of its moral example.

Eugene Debs's significance as an opponent of war lay in the strength of his convictions and the appeal of his personality. A romantic and a preacher, rather than a politician, there was little practical leadership in his exhortations. Like most other Socialists of his day, he opposed war because he believed that it resulted from capitalist greed and rivalry. Impulsive, emotional, and often inconsistent, he had little real understanding of international affairs. Yet his sincerity was rarely questioned, even by those who considered his attacks on American participation in the World War to be treasonable. His undeviating adherence to moral standards, his generosity, and his genial and unaffected friendliness made of him one of the most popular figures in the history of American radicalism. No more fitting tribute could be paid him than that offered on the occasion of his death by Victor Berger, the first Socialist to be elected to Congress: "He loved his neighbor better than himself."[56]

CHAPTER TWO

MORRIS HILLQUIT

(1869–1933)

LOGICIAN OF SOCIAL REVOLUTION

> I am an American, if that means a citizen who seeks
> for the greatest welfare of his country, of his fellow
> citizens. . . . I stand behind the President when I
> honestly believe he is right, and only then. I stand
> behind the people all the time.
>
> —Morris Hillquit, as quoted in the
> *New York Times,* 30 October 1917.

While Debs was the heart and the soul of American Socialism,
he was never its intellectual leader. The "brains" of the movement
was Morris Hillquit, a well-to-do lawyer who spoke a dozen
languages, was five times a candidate for Congress (in 1906,
1908, 1916, 1918, and 1920), and ran for mayor of New York
City in 1917 and 1932. Hillquit's prominence in the party
derived neither from any great capacity for mass leadership nor
from an ability to inspire love, but rather from his powers as a
logician and his solid knowledge of Marxist thought—rare qualities in a movement which subsisted largely on emotionalism and
was highly susceptible to passing theoretical fads. While admittedly less of a symbol to American Socialists than other men
have been, the astute intelligence that Hillquit demonstrated
at international Socialist conferences earned him a reputation
on a level with the esteem bestowed on such European leaders
as Jean Jaurès, August Bebel, and Eduard Bernstein.[1]

Born in 1869 of Jewish parentage in Riga, Russia, Morris Hill-kowitz (the family name was legally changed later to Hillquit) emigrated to the United States in 1886 and spent the next decade on New York's Lower East Side. Before graduating in 1893 from the law school of the University of the City of New York, he worked for a time as business manager, associate editor, and poet for the *Arbeiter Zeitung,* the first American Yiddish newspaper.[2]

It was during his stay on the East Side—among whose inhabitants could be found proponents of nearly every known school of social, economic, or religious thought—that Hillquit gained his introduction to Socialism. He joined the Socialist Labor Party at the age of eighteen and became acquainted with Socialist literature and the organizational problems of the trade union movement while serving as a clerk in the party's office. In 1899, when the party split, he was one of the leaders of the faction which favored a broad base for Socialism and—in contradiction to Daniel DeLeon's belief in keeping the movement "pure"—advocated cooperation with such established labor organizations as the American Federation of Labor. In 1901 Hillquit was among those who joined Debs and other Social Democracy people in creating the Socialist Party of America. From then on, perhaps more than any other individual, he represented typical American Socialist thought, seeking through speeches and a steady output of articles, pamphlets, and books to interpret Socialism both for his colleagues and for the general public. Always more practical than Debs, he worked constantly to adapt Socialist doctrine to the needs of the native American situation. And it was largely his reasoned, thorough groundwork that established party policies.

Although once denounced as a "Red Anarchist" by evangelist Billy Sunday, Hillquit was by both temperament and outlook far removed from the extremism which such a label implies. A "centrist," belonging to neither the right nor left wings of his party, he believed that Socialism would come gradually, through social evolution and by political means, rather than by revolution. As a consequence, he was frequently an object of criticism in "the camp of the revolution," where, according to Max Eastman, he was regarded as "the symbol and sum-total of 'compro-

mise,' 'reformism,' 'opportunism,' the institutional selling-out
of the straight Marxian program of class war." Leon Trotsky,
for example, considered Hillquit "A Babbitt of Babbitts . . . , the
ideal Socialist leader for successful dentists." And Joseph Freeman suspected him of conspiring with the capitalists to betray
the workers. Yet, as a centrist, Hillquit was representative of
most members of the party, and he, in fact, struggled as ener-
getically against the piecemeal reform of certain American labor
leaders as he did against the extremist doctrines of the Communist Party.[3]

Besides his work as a Socialist theoretician, practical politician,
and semi-official party spokesman, Hillquit was prominent in a
number of Socialist clubs and educational societies, took an
active part in trade union organization, and devoted his career
as an attorney to left-wing causes. Among other things, he
served as one of the organizers of the United Hebrew Trades;
defended the anarchist editor Johann Most against a charge of
having endangered the public peace in a newspaper article
printed the day before President McKinley's assassination; was
a member of the negotiating committee that settled a major
strike which erupted in the garment industry during 1910; was
a trustee of the Rand School, a Socialist educational and propaganda institution founded in 1906; and sat for ten years on the
board of directors of the Intercollegiate Socialist Society (renamed the League for Industrial Democracy following the First
World War).

Like most other American Socialists, Hillquit regarded war as
an "anti-social institution" inherent in the nature of capitalism.
He took part in the formulation of the antiwar resolution adopted
at the Stuttgart Congress of the Second International in 1907
and repeated its essentials in his book *Socialism in Theory and
Practice* published two years later. His reply in 1911 to a letter
asking if he would accept nomination as Director of the New
York Peace Society is a succinct expression of the American
Socialists' stand on war in the years between the Stuttgart
Congress and 1917. "Modern wars are cool, calculated industrial
enterprises" which will disappear only with the disappearance
of the "diseased competitive system . . . which breeds them," he
wrote.

The organized Socialist movement of the world is relentlessly opposed to war. . . . Not only because wars are among the grossest relics of barbarism, and entail a criminal economic waste through standing armies and formidable navies, but more particularly because the suffering and miseries of wars fall almost exclusively upon the working class, and because militarism, with its inseparable companion—false patriotism—demoralize and debauch the public mind, and are a most formidable obstacle to true social progress.

When the First World War broke out in 1914, Hillquit was so dismayed by "the sudden collapse of human reason and the ugly sight of the world denuded of its thin veneer of civilization" that he became immediately one of the conflict's most determined and consistent opponents. Over the next four years his preoccupation with that great struggle was the central fact of his existence. As he later recounted in his autobiography, "the war affected my course of life and modified my whole outlook more deeply than any other event."[4]

Hillquit made his first public utterance on the war in an article published in the *American Socialist* of 5 September 1914 and subsequently reprinted in such newspapers as the *Omaha News* and the *San Francisco Bulletin.* The article revealed both his belief that the conflict was "the inevitable culmination of murderous European capitalism" and his fear of American involvement. "The barbarous institution of periodical international slaughter is the inseparable companion of the barbarous system of economic robbery called capitalism," he wrote. "The ruling classes of the United States are even today steering the ship of state towards a devastating world-war as surely and irresistibly as the ruling classes of Europe have been during the last generation."[5]

If there was one portion of the population in the war-stricken countries of Europe that Hillquit believed innocent of the "abominable rape of civilization," it was the Socialist working class and its representatives. "The Socialists are not responsible for the war," he stated in a speech of September 21 at New York's Harlem River Casino. The Socialist Parties in Europe could be charged with responsibility for the tragedy only if, instead of being in a minority, they had been in control. International Socialist solidarity has not been betrayed by our European colleagues, but rather has been "temporarily broken" by "the most

violent and virulent outbreak of capitalism ever witnessed in
history." As "the only living social force destined to put an
end to human slaughter," Hillquit went on to announce, "Socialism will emerge stronger than ever from this general European
cataclysm." Socialism's spirit "lives in all of us, here and in
Europe, and even before this fateful war will be over, it will
raise its defiant head again and inspire the workers of the world
to more intense human happiness and civilization." Seven months
later, Hillquit's optimism about the future of Socialism remained
sufficiently unshaken to permit the prediction that after the
war "the organizations of the workers will be more effective . . .
and their struggles more intense than ever before." "The Socialist movement as such has overcome many great trials," he
maintained in the *American Socialist.* "It will survive the war.
. . . International Socialism is imperishable."[6]

Hillquit's faith in Socialism's survival did not make him any
less active in his opposition to the war, however. In December
1914, his concern over "the spread of the militaristic spirit in
the United States" prompted him to cooperate with Jane
Addams, David Starr Jordan, and several other prominent
pacifists in forming the American League to Limit Armaments.
It was largely his insistence on having the league take a firm
stand or none at all that resulted in the adoption of a resolution
on December 18 stating that "the true policy of this country is
not to increase its land and sea forces, but to retain for productive and humanizing outlay the vast sums demanded for armaments." Moreover, it was Hillquit who prepared the peace program
adopted by the American Socialist Party in May 1915. From
an analysis of the program's content, it can be seen that Hillquit
anticipated by three years most of President Wilson's Fourteen
Points. Among other things, the manifesto urged that disarmament and international government be supported, that no
annexations or indemnities be permitted, and that the right of
political self-determination be respected.[7]

Yet Hillquit's strong antiwar sentiments never altered his
belief that good sense should govern the tactics used by American Socialists in voicing their opposition to the conflict. In contrast to Debs, for example, he was firmly against the proposal
that the party should call upon workers to declare a nation wide

general strike in the event that Congress declared war. And he labeled as "perfectly wild" Allan Benson's pet idea that a national referendum be held before an American declaration of war and that those who voted in favor of war be the first to go into the army. Any political group that adopted such an impracticable proposal, Hillquit wrote to the party's Bureau of Information director, would be made "a laughing stock." So strongly did he feel about the matter that he published his objections in the *New York Call* at the beginning of 1915. Not surprisingly, he was greatly distressed when Benson's proposal was included in the party's 1916 platform.[8]

It was also Hillquit's conviction that American Socialists should resist any temptation to take sides in the European war. He maintained in the *American Socialist* of 9 January 1915 that to claim the Allies were fighting for democracy was just as false and hypocritical as the contention that "the German sword has been drawn in the interests of 'culture.' " Far from being "a fight for sentiment or ideals," the struggle across the Atlantic

is a cold-blooded butchery for advantages and power, and let us not forget —advantages and power for the ruling classes of the warring nations. . . . A decisive victory on either side is likely to foster a spirit of military over-bearing and pseudo-patriotic exaltation on the part of the victorious countries, lasting resentment and increased military activity on the part of the defeated nations, and a general condition of pan-European irritation with a tendency to another, perhaps even more pernicious war.

Therefore, Hillquit concluded, "the most satisfactory solution. . . . lies in a draw, a cessation of hostilities from sheer exhaustion without determining anything." Only then, when it is unmistakably clear that all the death and destruction was in vain, "will this war remain forever accursed in the memory of men" and "will it lead the people of all nations to revolt against any repetition of this frightful experience and to revolt against the capitalist system which leads to such paroxysms of madness."

Ironically, both Hillquit's plea for Socialist neutrality and his subsequent defense in *Metropolitan* of the German Social-

ists' support of their government* were regarded by a number
of his colleagues as evidence of pro-Germanism. For example, his
friend George Herron, who considered that "a German victory
would mean the end of socialism for a long time to come,"
wrote him from Florence, Italy:

I do not think you are really as impartial as you imagine you are. You *are*
a pro-German. . . . No disinterested reader could possibly take your series
of articles in the *Metropolitan* for anything else than an apology for German social democracy. . . . If I did not know you at all, I should say that
you were not only an apologist for German socialism, but a sympathiser
with Germany in this struggle. Your neutrality or impartiality is a delusion.

Certain other Socialists, such as Louis Fraina, accused Hillquit
of "nationalistic bias." According to Fraina, Hillquit's article in
the February 1915 issue of *Metropolitan* was "in full agreement"
with those "reactionary elements of Bourgeois progressivism"
who called upon Socialists to be "realistic" as concerns the
problem of defense. "Morris Hillquit indulges in the identical
language and illusion: the lofty ideal of Socialism 'does not blind
the Socialists to the implacable realities of present-day conditions.' Hillquit refuses to say that Socialism is against armaments
and militarism." What Fraina neglected to acknowledge—perhaps
because to do so would have contradicted his image of Hillquit
as a spokesman for "Bourgeois progressivism"—was that the
Metropolitan article left little doubt as to either Socialism's opposition "to all wars between nations and within the nations"
or its stand that the only way to stop capitalist war was to overthrow capitalist governments. Still, one can readily understand
why a left-wing Socialist like Fraina might detect a "nationalistic bias" in Hillquit's rationale for supporting international,

---

*Beginning in December 1914, and ending in May 1915, Hillquit published in
Metropolitan a six-article series on "Socialism and War." In the March issue he revealed a benevolently understanding attitude toward not only the German Social
Democrats, with whom he was linked personally and politically, but also the French
and British Socialists. He condoned them all on the ground that in supporting their
governments in the war they had simply "yielded to the inexorable necessities of
the situation." ("How the Socialists Met the War," p. 46.)

rather than unilateral, disarmament: "It would be futile and foolish to preach disarmament to any nation while its neighbors and rivals are armed. . . . Under existing conditions each nation must be prepared to defend its integrity and independence against the rest of the world, and must maintain a strong military organization for that purpose."[9]

When the American Socialist Party's National Executive Committee had proposed in September 1914 that an international conference of Socialists be held in Washington, D. C., Hillquit had rejected the idea as "fantastic." "This is not the time, and Washington . . . is certainly not the place for such a conference," he complained in a letter to the party's national executive secretary. "As yet the Socialist parties in Europe are completely stunned by the sudden catastrophic events of the war and their activities are practically suspended. When the time will be ripe for such a gathering, it will certainly have to take place in Europe, probably in Holland or Denmark." Pointing out that a trip to the United States and back would take five or six weeks, he added that it would be "preposterous to expect the most active and influential men of the Socialist movement of Europe to leave their countries for that length of time at this critical juncture. . . . I fear our invitation will not only remain without response but will make us ridiculous in the eyes of the international Socialist movement." As it turned out, the conference was subsequently scheduled to convene in Copenhagen on 15 January 1915, and Hillquit was selected as his party's delegate. However, after learning at the last moment that the only other participants in the conference would be from Sweden, Norway, Denmark, and Holland, Hillquit decided not to attend. The concluding paragraph of his lengthy letter communicating that decision to the National Executive Committee is worth repeating, for it includes his perception of American Socialism's "mission":

. . . The voice of a general council of the Socialists of the neutral countries might be expected to carry considerable weight with their comrades on both sides of the conflict; to influence their mutual feelings during the war and to aid them in the formulation of a uniform programme in connection with the future negotiations of their respective countries. A purely local conference, such as the Copenhagen assembly will unfortunately be, can hardly be expected to have such an effect.Moreover, the four countries which will be represented at Copenhagen have certain specific local and sectional interests, which are not shared by the other neutral countries, and I am inclined to believe that the United States would be out of place in such a conference. The neutrality of the countries of Europe is not as absolute as that of the United States. Owing to their geographical positions, commercial interests, and racial ties, most European countries are some-what biased in favor of one or the other of the belligerent forces, and be-fore the war is over some of them may be drawn into the active conflict. The very fact that even the Socialists of all neutral countries refuse to meet in common conference at this time indicates that the feeling among the neutral nations is somewhat strained. America alone has no interest in this war except in its speedy termination, and American Socialists above all others must studiously avoid even the slightest appearance of bias or discrimination among their unfortunate comrades in Europe. This war will end sometime, and when it ends somebody will have to initiate the work of reconstructing the shattered International of the workers. This great task will logically fall to the Socialists of America, the Socialists of the most important and least concerned nation. I fear that this mission, the largest that will ever come to our movement, may be jeopardized by the participation in a somewhat one-sided conference, and therefore have concluded not to go to Copenhagen.[10]

Throughout 1915 Hillquit's views on the war were given wide circulation. He was interviewed both by Edward Marshall of the *New York Times* and by William Hard of *Everybody's* magazine; he publicly debated Republican Congressman Augustus P. Gardner of Massachusetts on the question "Must We Arm?"; his articles appeared in journals ranging from *Ford Hall Folks* to the *Yale Review;*[11] and he spoke before such groups as the Emergency Conference of Peace Forces and the American Acad-emy of Political and Social Science.[12]

It was in his April 1915 debate with Congressman Gardner that Hillquit first commented at any length on military prepar-edness. His response to Gardner's argument on behalf of a strong army and navy capable of fighting a serious war was that increased military strength was not only unnecessary, since the United States was in no real danger, but would mean "the brutalization of the country":

The argument of modern American militarism . . . is based on a colossal fallacy. The United States is not in danger of war. It has never been safer from hostile attack than it is at this period. . . . The main causes of the great European war were artificial political boundaries, historical grudges, commercial rivalry, imperialism, and militarism. . . . In the United States we find a complete absence of factors that naturally make for war, and a happy combination of conditions calculated to ensure lasting peace. . . . The propaganda for increased armaments at this time is pregnant with the gravest menace to the well-being and security of the nation. . . . Strenuous preparation "against war" means not only invitation of war, it means the brutalization of the country. . . . The United States can never become a first-class military power. Let us center our ambition, our hope and aspiration on making our country the first great peace power of the world.

Early in 1916 Hillquit traveled to the nation's capital, where he visited President Wilson in the White House and appeared before the Foreign Affairs Committee of the House of Representatives in an attempt to win support for the Socialist Party's proposal that the United States convoke a congress of neutral nations to offer mediation to the belligerents in Europe. That his efforts in this connection were of no avail may have influenced his subsequent decision to accept nomination as the Socialist candidate for Congress in the twentieth district of New York. A private citizen might urge American mediation in the war, but it was the country's elected representatives who had the power to put such a program into action.[13]

Although Hillquit was unsuccessful in his bid for Congress (losing by only 150 votes), he used to good advantage the opportunities afforded by the campaign to attract public attention to the Socialists' view of the war. In accepting his party's nomination, for example, he issued a statement devoted almost entirely to the theme of capitalism's responsibility for "the heavy tragedy of blood-stained Europe." Could anything better demonstrate America's "need of a complete and immediate change of the existing social and economic institutions" than the debacle across the Atlantic? The ruling classes of this country were already "busy at work cultivating the deadly germs of strife and bloodshed," Hillquit warned. With similar devotion to the antiwar cause, he took advantage of a hotly worded editorial in the *New York Times* accusing him of being wholly devoid of patriotism and of dwelling in "a fool's paradise" to attack the proponents of preparedness. "Patriotism," he informed a mass meeting at the Harlem Star Casino on 22 October 1916, is "very much abused" by the militarists. "Patriotism . . . means nothing if it does not mean love of the people. True patriotism expresses itself in honest efforts to enhance the happiness and welfare of the great masses of the people." Hence, it is not those who strive for peace, but those who "pave the way for strife and war with foreign nations" who are "thoroughly unpatriotic." America will best be served by an end to the bloodshed in Europe. True patriotism lies not in military preparedness, but in mediation efforts.[14]

Hillquit ceased his pleas for American mediation early in 1917, when the leaders of Germany decided that the Central Powers could force a favorable decision in the war by means of unrestricted submarine assault on neutral commerce trading across the high seas to the Allied nations. He did, however, continue to insist on American neutrality, arguing that the wrongs inflicted on this country by the German undersea initiative were not as great as those which would result from intervention in the European war. "If in normal times the German Government should go out of its way to destroy American life or property," he told a reporter for the *New York Times*,

it might furnish a proper cause for war. But with Germany now engaged in a life and death combat and fighting on sea and with all available means which only despair can dictate; if, under those conditions any of our citizens deliberately leave a place of safety and venture into the arena of the fight and get hurt, we have no righteous cause for war. The rule that sensible individuals follow with regard to street brawls is the rule for nations in the matter of war.

Such reasoning may have been sound, but it was hardly warmly received. An increasing number of Americans not only regarded Germany's "overt acts" as ample justification for going to war, but tended to agree with patriots in the mold of Henry A. Wise Wood that "parasites" like Morris Hillquit ("who seeks to teach Americans their duty and speaks with a strong foreign accent") were "a dangerous element" in American society.[15]

On 4 March 1917, when the Manhattan Socialists gathered to discuss their stand at the forthcoming national convention, which was to meet in April for the purpose of clarifying the

Socialist Party's position on the war, Hillquit had occasion to demonstrate that he was less "dangerous" than Wise supposed. Although the Manhattan group was united in opposition to American intervention, a "left" wing under the guidance of Leon Trotsky favored responding to a declaration of war with civil violence. Hillquit led the "moderates" in calling for a policy more in keeping with the tradition of American parliamentarianism. Expressing the opinion that "we should be asses to tell members of Local New York that they must risk death and imprisonment rather than join the army," he argued that an effort to turn the war into a struggle between classes would be wholly unsuited to the American scene. The majority of delegates agreed with him. Trotsky's tactics were rejected in favor of a resolution which, while pledging Socialist opposition to the war, omitted any encouragement of actions likely to result in violence, including strikes against mobilization and conscription. Trotsky would remember his defeat as one of a number of disappointing experiences that caused him to regard most American Socialists as "successful and semi-successful doctors, lawyers, dentists, engineers, and the like who . . . tolerate all ideas, provided they do not undermine their traditional authority, and do not threaten—God forbid!—their personal comfort."[16]

Hillquit likewise played a dominant role at the national convention in St. Louis, which opened on the day following the American declaration of war. He served briefly as the convention's temporary chairman, delivered the keynote address, and joined Charles Ruthenberg and Algernon Lee in writing the report known subsequently as the St. Louis Proclamation. In each of these capacities he demonstrated the same realistic approach to Socialist activity evident in his earlier confrontation with Trotsky. It was at his urging, for example, that the convention's Committee on War and Militarism excluded "general pacifist statements" from its majority report. "We are not pacifists," Hillquit reminded his fellow committee members. "Ours is a militant, revolutionary organization. We all fight within the nation for the interests of the working class. We will defend the rights of the workers whenever an attack is made. If we are ready to fight the ruling class, economically and politically, within the nation, do we draw the line outside the nation?" To

take abstract positions and to maintain that the workers have
no country and will not defend themselves if attacked, he stated,
would be foolish: "Our country is a certain political organization within which we live and act. Our very object of seeking to
conquer this country shows we are trying to make this nation
ours. It would be silly on our part to say that under no circumstances would we defend ourselves or our country."[17]

One result of Hillquit's prominent part in formulating the
St. Louis Proclamation was an invitation to write the introduction to Alexander Trachtenberg's documentary history *The
American Socialists and the War,* a task which he accepted
readily as an opportunity to dispel any confusion about the
party's attitude. Another, less welcome, consequence was that
he was singled out for verbal abuse by a number of prominent
colleagues who disagreed sharply with the party's condemnation
of the war "as a crime against the people of the United States
and against the nations of the world." With the exception of
his old friend W. J. Ghent, however, most of Hillquit's critics
caused him little personal distress, and he responded to them
forcibly. For instance, when John Spargo labeled him a "pro-
German" who favored a separate peace between Russia and
the Central Powers, Hillquit sent letters to both the *New York
Times* and the *New York Call* in which he branded the accusation as not only "impertinent" but a "perversion of facts."
"I do not know of a single American Socialist of any standing
in his party who favors a separate peace," he wrote. "The vast
majority of the Socialists in the United States heartily accept
the program of their Russian comrades for a speedy and general
peace. . . ." Shortly thereafter, in answer to an announcement
by Spargo, Allan Benson, and two other Socialists that the "pro-
German sympathies" of the St. Louis Proclamation might cause
them to leave the party, he released a statement to the effect
that the "dictates of common decency" required such resigna-
tions, since the men in question held opinions hostile to the
party.[18]

Dissident Socialists like Spargo and Benson could do little
more than voice their displeasure. The government, on the other
hand, had the power to disrupt Hillquit's plans—a power which it
chose to exercise in May 1917 when the American Socialist Party

delegated Hillquit, Algernon Lee, and Victor Berger to take part in an international Socialist conference in Stockholm summoned to discuss how to end the war. The three men were prevented from attending the conference by Secretary of State Lansing, who, characterizing the assembly as "a cleverly directed German war move," disapproved their applications for passports.[19] Hillquit went to Washington to appeal the Secretary's decision, arguing that the Socialist peace program—far from favoring Germany—was in full accord with the war aims announced by President Wilson on May 22. But his efforts were in vain. Much to the delight of those who believed that the Stockholm conference was "the most dangerous of all the Kaiser's Plots,"[20] the State Department persisted in its refusal to issue passports. Had the department acted otherwise, the *New York Times* editorialized on August 8, "aid and comfort" would have been given to the enemy. "The Socialist Party of the United States is openly disloyal. . . . The members of the party who are loyal Americans in thought and feeling have withdrawn from it. The remnant is very largely pro-German, and altogether anti-American."

Following the denial of peace efforts on an international scale, Hillquit increased his antiwar activities on the home front. As one of the organizers of the Peoples' Council of America for Democracy and the Terms of Peace, he allied himself with non-Socialists like David Starr Jordan, president of Stanford University and a pacifist whose opposition to war dated back to the Spanish-American conflict. Ironically, Hillquit's support of the Council's efforts to persuade the government to negotiate a rapid and "democratic" peace resulted in his being attacked not only by Samuel Gompers's labor-loyalty agency, the American Alliance for Labor and Democracy,[21] but also by left-wing Socialists who regarded the Council as a "bourgeois pacifist" organization with which the working class had nothing in common. Apparently, the party's left wing found particularly objectionable the Council's failure to mention what the Socialists felt were the economic causes of the war, and the necessity of eradicating these causes.[22]

In the summer of 1917 Hillquit was nominated as the Socialist candidate for mayor of New York City on a platform opposing conscription. The ensuing campaign was among the most dramatic in American history. Night after night there were street meetings charged with a passion rare in American politics, and at the contest's height Socialist rallies filled Madison Square Garden a half dozen or more times to its capacity of 15,000. Hillquit was supported enthusiastically not only by every available Socialist speaker in the city and the five daily Socialist papers, but also by a variety of liberal and pacifist organizations ranging from the Irish Progressive League to the Collegiate League for Hillquit, an association of college graduates organized by Randolph Bourne and independent of any political party. Although this support was not sufficient to bring Hillquit victory, he did surprisingly well, capturing twenty-two percent of the vote and placing third in a four-cornered race.* The sting of his defeat was further lessened by the fact that as a result of the large vote the Socialists sent seven aldermen to City Hall, ten assemblymen to Albany, and elected a municipal-court judge. That there were also large votes favoring Socialist candidates in many other cities made the wartime election of 1917 the high-water mark of Socialist political strength in American history.[23]

There is no doubt that Hillquit saw the issue of war and peace as the leading factor in the campaign. On September 23, in a speech at Madison Square Garden announcing his acceptance of the Socialist Party's nomination, he told a crowd of 12,000: "The municipal election in this city will be the only great political contest in the United States since our entry in the war. It will offer the first real opportunity to the greatest community in the country to express its sentiments on war and peace." In the weeks that followed, he repeated this perception of the campaign's significance time and again—emphasizing that a Socialist victory in New York would be a clear mandate to the government to open immediate negotiations for a general peace and noting that America alone was in a position to determine whether the World War would continue or whether there would be a permanent peace.[24]

---

*The winner, Democrat John F. Hylan, polled 313,956 votes; the Fusion candidate, incumbent Mayor John P. Mitchel, received 155,497 votes; and the official Republican candidate, William F. Bennett, finished last with 56,438. Hillquit's vote of 145,332 represented an increase of more than 400 percent over what Charles Edward Russell had polled as the Socialist candidate in 1913.

William Hard's charge in the *New Republic* of October 6 that Hillquit favored "an immediate separate peace, a withdrawal by America," was wholly untrue. On the contrary, he insisted on a general, negotiated peace for all belligerents, based on the following points: no forcible annexations or punitive indemnities; the free development of all nations and nationalities; a guarantee of the permanence of peace resting upon the principle of universal disarmament; and an international organization for the settlement of disputes. "We want peace, and early peace," he told an audience in Bryant Hall on October 22,

> but let me repeat again what we cannot repeat too often: We do not stand for a separate peace, which would save our own skins and leave the unfortunate nations of Europe to their own destinies. We want a general, negotiated, and permanent peace, which would bring relief and blessing to the peoples of all countries involved in this insane and disastrous war.

Indeed, it was Hillquit's conviction that America's entry into the war had betrayed the people of Europe ("They were expecting peace, . . . and then suddenly we joined the world conflagration . . . we, the one power strong enough, fresh enough, to be in a position to determine the fate of mankind. . . ."), and that for America now to simply withdraw from the conflict would constitute a second betrayal.[25]

At first, Hillquit's pleas on behalf of a prompt and general peace provoked little response from the camps of the other candidates. However, the announcement in late October that his devotion to peace would not permit him to purchase liberty bonds engendered a torrent of invective that continued unabated throughout the remainder of the campaign. Mayor Mitchel was joined by the Chamber of Commerce, the Business Men's League, and the Lawyers Club in asserting that any man who refused to buy liberty bonds when he could so obviously afford them* was not fit to be a citizen of the United States; Theodore Roose-

---

*Although Hillquit's personal wealth was not a central issue in the campaign, following his refusal to buy Liberty Bonds the *New York Times* (28 October 1917) ran a character sketch entitled "Rich Mr. Hillquit, Poor Man's Candidate." The article pointed out that "the candidate of the proletariat" owned corporation stocks and lived in "an exclusive apartment" on Riverside Drive. "It has been said that he is a wealthier man than any of his three opponents."

velt denounced Hillquit as the "ally of the Hun in world politics" and climaxed an impassioned speech at Madison Square Garden on November 1 with "Yellow calls to yellow"; Charles Evans Hughes and former Ambassador to Turkey Oscar Straus publicly referred to Hillquit as "treasonable"; the *New York Herald* ran a page one cartoon depicting a hook-nosed man named "Hillkowitz or Hillquitter" waving a flag labeled "Peace at any price" at a smiling "Kaiser"; the *New York Times,* in endorsing Mitchel, labeled Hillquit "the German candidate"; even the liberal *New York World* attacked Hillquit, declaring in an election-day editorial: "Today's election will determine whether New York is a traitor town . . . or an American town devoted to American ideals and pledged without reservation to the war policies of the United States government."[26]

Hillquit was understandably distressed by the attacks on him, but—except for occasional barbed comments directed at Theodore Roosevelt, whom he believed to be "the most demoralizing influence" in American political life—he chose not to respond in kind. Although he regarded the allegations of his critics as responsible for such things as that he alone among the candidates was prohibited from speaking at Camp Upton (a military training center at Yaphank, Long Island), he operated under the assumption that he had little to gain from engaging in personal polemics. Hence, he answered charges of treason and pro-Germanism firmly, but with a polite restraint and "gentlemanliness" sufficient to earn him editorial praise in the *Nation.*[27]

In later describing the "heavy atmosphere of hate and terrorism" in which he moved during the campaign, Hillquit identified as especially annoying the presence at his public meetings of stenographers from the United States district attorney's office, who busily took down every word he uttered. Yet he refused to be intimidated into refraining from criticizing the war. Rather, he used his experience as an orator and his knowledge of the law "to steer safely between dangerous patriotic cliffs," skillfully avoiding language that might serve as a basis for indictment under the Espionage Act. As his campaign associate Louis Lochner would recall more than three decades later in a letter to Robert Iversen, "Hillquit was a keen attorney and it was delightful to watch how close he would come to the point where a zealous district attorney might accuse him of subversive utterances."[28]

Hillquit spoke most bluntly in voicing his disapproval of government efforts to enforce uniformity of opinion on the war. Long a defender of civil liberties, he found it incomprehensible that a so-called "war for democracy" abroad could be accompanied by attempts to stifle legitimate political criticism at home. As he saw it, the "real patriots" were not those who, like Theodore Roosevelt, demanded "the formation of vigilantes to suppress hostile . . . views," but those who supported the Constitution—a document which, unfortunately, was fast being reduced to "a mere 'scrap of paper' " by "the breaking up of peaceful meetings, the invasion of homes, and the suppression of newspapers." "The Constitution of the United States was made for all times, times of war and times of peace," he affirmed at a dinner meeting of the Collegiate League for Hillquit. "A democracy which can be taken away from the people for one single minute by any one man or group of men, no matter how great or how wise, is no longer a democracy." So strong was Hillquit's conviction that Americans had "the right"—and, indeed, "the duty"—to discuss peace, that he interrupted his busy campaign schedule to travel to Washington in an unsuccessful effort to prevent Postmaster General Albert S. Burleson (to whom he referred publicly as "a prolific accuser, a merciless judge, and a prompt executioner") from revoking the second-class mailing privileges of the *New York Call.*[29]

Ironically, in the months following the campaign, when the government began to crack down and restrict free speech by bringing indictments under the Espionage Act, Hillquit would have reason to look back upon the 1917 election as having offered critics of the war relative freedom to voice their opposition. Moreover, before much time had passed, Hillquit would learn as well that he had been unduly optimistic in asserting during a post-election interview that the great increase in the Socialist vote proved that the Socialist Party had been established as "an important and permanent factor" in the politics of New York City. As was pointed out in an editorial appraisal of the election by the *New Republic,* "the proportion of convinced Socialists in the Hillquit vote was minor." Persons who voted for him did so mainly because they were either opposed to the war or to the manner in which its civil relations were being handled. "To vote for Hillquit was the only practicable method of protesting against any of the administration policies."[30]

Although the strenuous campaign of 1917 left Hillquit exhausted, he immediately assumed a heavy burden of legal work, not only successfully defending Frank Harris (editor of *Pearson's* magazine) and Scott Nearing against espionage charges, but also serving as chief counsel for the defense in the first *Masses* trial. He was scheduled as well to take part in the second *Masses* trial and in the cases of Eugene Debs and Victor Berger,* but was forced to withdraw when he learned in the summer of 1918 that he was suffering from pulmonary tuberculosis. On his return to active professional life at the beginning of 1920, he fought unsuccessfully the expulsion of five Socialist members of the New York Assembly.[31]

During the winter of 1917–1918, in the wake of the Bolshevik takeover in Russia, there was a noticeable change in the attitude of many American radicals toward the war. The Kaiser's rejection of peace terms seemingly offering sympathy and consideration to the Bolsheviks, together with the negotiations which culminated in the Carthaginian peace forced by Germany upon the revolutionary government of Russia at Brest-Litovsk, combined to create in antiwar circles feelings of increased friendliness toward the Allies and of greater hostility toward the Central Powers. That Hillquit shared these feelings, at least in part, is evident from a comment he made to an audience of Socialists in late February, following the collapse of the Bolshevik "peace offensive": "It is now clearer than ever that Prussian and Austrian junkerdom is the foe of liberty and peace." Likewise, in responding on March 2 to the demand by the Jewish Socialist League for a special convention to put the Socialist Party "back of the government and unequivocally for the prosecution of the war," he acknowledged that the time might come when American Socialists would have to advocate "crushing . . . the Junkers

---

*Berger came to the United States from Austria in 1878 and helped organize the Socialist Party. He became editor of the *Milwaukee Leader*, served in Congress from 1911 to 1913, and late in 1918 was tried for violating the Espionage Act. Although Berger was found guilty and sentenced to twenty years' imprisonment, the United States Supreme Court ruled in 1921 that the trial judge should have granted a change of venue. As a consequence, the case was dismissed and the charges were officially dropped by the government in February 1923.

by military force." Yet the allegation of historian Christopher Lasch that Hillquit offered his services to the government as a propagandist is misleading. While it is true that he believed the Allied peace proposals worthy of support, he voted with the majority when the National Executive Committee of the Socialist Party met in August 1918 and rejected a proposal that the strict antiwar attitude of the St. Louis Proclamation be modified. Moreover, he never forgave President Wilson, "the apostle of the 'new freedom,' " for having "revived the medieval institutions of the inquisition of speech, thought, and conscience."[32]

The revolution in Russia not only served as an important factor in causing Hillquit to look more favorably upon an Allied victory, but also intensified in him the belief that a better civilization—a world of brotherhood and good will and peace—would emerge from the battlefields of Europe. That Russia had "broken away from the old capitalist moorings" and "turned a new page in history" was to him proof that the war had "hastened the revolution." "The historian of the next generation," he wrote in 1919, "will designate our war not as The Great War, nor as the World War, but as the War of the Social Revolution."[33]

Perhaps surprisingly, in view of his past insistence on a permanent international organization to adjust disputes between potential belligerents,[34] Hillquit's reaction to the League of Nations was at first highly critical. He described the League in September 1919 as an "Executive Committee of imperialistic governments" which had no other aims than the protection of "mutual plunder," the subversion of proletarian governments, and the suppression of revolution. "The so-called League of Nations," he complained, "marks the final stages of capitalist domination, the transfer of the class struggle from national battlefields to the international arena."[35] Over the next several years, however, Hillquit's attitude changed markedly. Indeed, in a public debate with Clarence Darrow at the beginning of 1926, he took the affirmative side on the question "Shall the United States enter the League of Nations and the World Court?" While acknowledging the League's "iniquitous origin," its "many and grave shortcomings in constitution and practical operations," and the "sinister motives" of some of its advocates, he argued that its status as the only international organization of governments designed, at least ostensibly, to avert or minimize wars made the membership of the United States a necessity. "I am deeply convinced that our participation . . . will aid the cause of peace and the cause of world justice," he commented. "The League of Nations was undoubtedly intended by the great reactionary powers . . . as a new instrument of world enslavement," but "the working people under Socialist leadership will see to it that this weapon is . . . turned into an instrument of world liberation."[36]

Although Hillquit devoted the closing years of his life largely to the complexities of left-wing politics and to the responsibilities associated with his membership in various Socialist clubs and educational organizations, he never ceased referring to the First World War as an object lesson in the folly and inhumanity of capitalist civilization. Like Eugene Debs, he remained to the end* an outspoken advocate of peace through Socialism, convinced that military conflicts between nations might be postponed by arbitration and the abolition of armaments, but that they would disappear only with the disappearance of the capitalist system which spawned them. "Modern wars . . . are made by the ruling classes and fought by the masses. They bring wealth and power to the privileged few and suffering, death and desolation to the many. . . ."[37]

---

*Hillquit died of tuberculosis on 7 October 1933, less than a year after his second unsuccessful race as the Socialist Party's candidate for mayor of New York City.

CHAPTER THREE

MAX EASTMAN

(1883–1969)

RENAISSANCE RADICAL

It takes more solitary courage to live and die a world
heretic . . . , than it does to risk an emblazoned death
amid a nation's applause.

—From Max Eastman's essay "Patriotism:
A Primitive Ideal," 1906.

Today I saw a face—it was a beak,
That peered, with pale round yellow vapid eyes,
Above the bloody muck that had been lips
And teeth and chin. A plodding doctor poured
Some water through a rubber down a hole
He made in that black bag of horny blood.
The beak revived. It smiled—as chickens smile.
The doctor hopes he'll find the man a tongue
To brag with, and I hope he'll find it, too.

—"At the Red Cross Hospital," a poem
written by Max Eastman during a visit to
Paris in 1915.

Few historians are likely to quarrel with Milton Cantor's
recent judgment that the American writer and editor Max Eastman was neither "a great literary figure, nor one of the giants of
American radicalism." Yet, at the time the United States entered
the First World War, Eastman—then in his fifth year as editor
of the *Masses*—was probably the nation's best-known literary
radical. Talented as an orator as well as a writer, and a man whose

personal charms and skill as a propagandist were such that he could speak to strikers one day and tap bankers for funds to defend anarchists the next, he seemed to many Americans in 1917 the embodiment of "the New Spirit of the intelligentsia in rebellion against convention."[1]

Eastman was born in Canandaigua, New York, the youngest child of two Congregational ministers, and spent the latter years of his childhood in Elmira, the home of Mark Twain. He graduated from Mercersburg Academy in 1900 as class valedictorian, with the highest scholastic average in the history of the school. In 1905 he took his B.A. degree at Williams College (where he edited the college yearbook, won prizes for oratory, and was elected to Phi Beta Kappa) and subsequently did graduate work in philosophy, psychology, and political science at Columbia University. From 1907 to 1911 he served at Columbia as John Dewey's assistant and taught logic and philosophy. Although he fulfilled all the requirements for a Ph.D. degree in philosophy, he chose not to receive it, professing a dislike of "such ornaments."[2]

In 1912, the same year that he announced his affiliation with the Socialist Party, Eastman became editor of the *Masses,* replacing the magazine's founder, Piet Vlag. Over the next five years he transformed what had been under Vlag a rather mild organ of moderate Socialism into "the Bible of the radical avante-garde." Later recalled by John Dos Passos as "the only magazine I ever had any use for," Eastman's *Masses* became a model of imaginative journalism—exuberant, impertinent, humorous,* always "fearless and young and laughing at everything solemn and conservative," the "rallying center . . . for almost everything that was then alive and irreverent in American culture." Its contributors included such luminaries of the cultural-radical community as Vachel Lindsay, William Carlos Williams, Louis Untermeyer, Randolph Bourne, John Reed, and Upton Sinclair.[3]

---

*The magazine's humor was sometimes unintentional. The manner in which its artists depicted the "proletariat" is a case in point. As noted by Oscar Ameringer, perhaps the American labor movement's greatest humorist: "In the *Masses* all miners were six feet two inches tall, had the chests, arms and legs of gorillas, and were forever breaking chains around their bulging biceps." (*If You Don't Weaken* [New York: Henry Holt, 1940], p. 411.)

Early in 1918, not long after the *Masses* was forced to cease publication because of its opposition to United States involvement in the war, Eastman and his sister, Crystal, founded the *Liberator*. Eastman edited this new journal for three years, while his sister served as business manager. Although less flamboyant and more studiedly political than the *Masses* had been, the *Liberator* lived up to the great tradition of its predecessor. Until the beginning of 1921, when the original editorial board disintegrated, it not only had much the same personnel and a similar format, but was—in Eastman's words—"distinguished by a complete freedom in art and poetry and fiction and criticism." H. L. Mencken regarded it "the best magazine in America. . . . It is informing, it is good tempered, it is often brilliant."[4]

While visiting Russia from 1922 to 1924 Eastman developed a close association with Leon Trotsky, whom he regarded as "head and shoulders above the other Bolsheviks, both in personal force and revolutionary understanding." It was Eastman's book *Since Lenin Died* (1925) which first revealed to the world the manner in which Trotsky's authority had been undermined by Stalin and his fellow "triumvirs," Zinoviev and Kamenev. In later years, after Trotsky went to Mexico, Eastman served as the Russian exile's literary agent in the United States.[5]

As time passed, Eastman became not only increasingly critical of Stalinism, but also more and more skeptical of Marxism as a "science." His last pro–Soviet lecture was in 1933. The following year he published *Artists in Uniform,* an account of the regimentation and censorship of arts and letters in the Soviet Union. The best of his books attacking Marxism as unscientific, *Marxism: Is It a Science?*, appeared in 1940, the same year as *Stalin's Russia and the Crisis in Socialism*—a book in which he argued that the failure of Socialism in Russia was due more to Lenin's methods than to Stalin's character.[6]

In subsequent years, having deserted for good the "camp of the revolution," Eastman served as a roving editor for the *Reader's Digest* and lectured across the United States and in foreign countries. Among his best-known nonpolitical books are *Enjoyment of Poetry* (1913), *Enjoyment of Laughter* (1936), and two volumes of autobiography: *Enjoyment of Living* (1948) and *Love and Revolution: My Journey Through an Epoch* (1964).

He died in Barbados, British West Indies, on 25 March 1969.

Although Eastman reversed many of his views over the course of the years—moving from spokesman of the radical left to champion of free enterprise—he never changed his mind about the folly of America's participation in the First World War. As he noted just five years before his death:

In 1937 George Gallup took a nation-wide poll on the question: "Do you think it was a mistake for the United States to enter the World War?" Seventy percent of those questioned voted *yes*. I agreed with them then, and though I supported our entrance into the Second World War, I have never changed my mind about the First.[7]

Eastman rarely exercised restraint in describing the negative features of warfare. "War," he wrote while serving as editor of the *Masses*, "is essentially a competition in murder," a competition which "makes it impossible to live" or "even to die for a noble purpose." Moreover, it is "the destroyer of liberty." Thus those who are loyal to the rights of human life and to the hope of liberty, he insisted, "will be neutral, whether the government goes to war or not." Yet Eastman made it clear that he was not a pacifist, but rather one "averse to fighting for a negative result, or an abstraction, as the soldiers do." As he saw it, there are two kinds of wars—wars of "national honor" and wars that are "morally necessary," that "have a great prize in view, human liberty, namely, and the right to live and bear children." While both kinds are admittedly a "denial of life," the latter—"class wars"— are merely a "defense against exploitation," and therefore have "every moral sanction conceivable." Hopefully, people might "cease to murder altogether," but, if not, then let them have wars "not of nation against nation, but of men against men, struggling to some real end." Let "the thundering feet of millions that go forth to die for the nation's honor" be replaced by the "positive program and policy" of those who, like the members of the I. W. W., advocate "sabotage and violence" as "excellent tactics in the fight of an oppressed class against its oppressors."[8]

Although Eastman readily admitted that commercial rivalry was among the causes of the First World War, he rejected the contention of most Socialists that the conflict was wholly capitalist-inspired. For him the war was neither "a result of capitalism," nor even a phenomenon "of peculiar interest to the business class," but rather "a result of group psychology in a pugnacious animal." "People do not go to war for their property," he insisted. "They go to war for their country. . . . The motive to patriotic fighting is not a mere derivative from business interest; it is a native impulse of our constitutions." The "fighting identification of self with a nation" may be "the most banal of stupid human idol-worships," but it is nonetheless "a disposition that lies fixed in the hereditary structure of all civilized races." Arguing against it is "like arguing against gravitation."[9]

Given the "unalterable facts" of man's bellicose and herd instincts, Eastman believed that the only way to end war was to alter the environment in such a manner as "to offer new objects for these instincts to adhere to, and similar but less disastrous functions for them to perform." While he urged Socialists and other opponents of war to engage in antimilitary propaganda, he was convinced that true and lasting peace would come only when mankind succeeded in forming "an international federation, not unlike our federation of American states." "Wars will arise between nations so long as the instinct of fighting loyalty is allowed to attach exclusively to nations," he wrote in 1916.

And as soon as, and in proportion as, we offer to that instinct larger groups to which it may attach itself, wars among nations will become less and less likely. We shall eliminate national war by international union. . . . That is all you can do with a trait that is hereditary. You can't ignore it, you can't mortify it, you can't preach it away, and you can't reason it away. It is there like a mouth which is bound to be fed. But you can feed it a slightly different food. You can offer it a different object to cling to.[10]

What set Eastman even further apart from orthodox Socialists was his contention that the chief force in accomplishing world federation would not be the workers but the capitalists. Socialists are "wrong in thinking that modern war is desirable from the standpoint of the capitalist," he argued. On the contrary, the awareness that "war doesn't pay"—that it is "bad business"—makes international capital "the greatest power on earth against war." The first task of the Socialists should be to join the bourgeois movement to eliminate war by world federation. The "gentle crime of abolishing capitalism through the class struggle" may be attended to later.

Consistent with such views, the *Masses'* outspoken editor was highly complimentary toward President Wilson's efforts to establish the League of Nations. Yet his praise ended when it became clear that Wilson's federation would exclude Bolshevik Russia. Notwithstanding Eastman's repeated assertions that he found war more abhorrent than capitalist exploitation, by the end of 1918 he was lamenting that the proposed league promised to become little more than a capitalist device to suppress Socialist revolutions. "Better no movement of the governments whatever," he complained in May, 1919, "than this deliberate attempt to settle and establish empire amid the instinctive beginnings of international consciousness."[11]

Much like Morris Hillquit, Eastman considered it an exercise in futility to attempt to identify any particular nation as bearing principal responsibility for the outbreak of war in 1914. Maintaining in the *Masses* of March 1916 that militarism was "not a trait of any race or nation," he appealed to those Americans who professed to hate militarism not to be deluded into imagining that it was Germany they were hating. What they were really hating, he explained, was what they would themselves become if the dreams of their "munition-makers and gold-braided patriots" were realized. "Do not let them make you hate Germany. Hate militarism. And hate it hardest where you have the best chance to do something against it. Hate it here. 'America first!' "

That Eastman insisted "there is no such thing as German militarism," however, did not prevent him from deploring German despotism. He regarded that nation's "feudal and absolute military oppression" as "the most abominable monster in Europe." So intense was his distaste for the "archaic rulers and all the retinue of physical and intellectual lackeys" who dominated the "pleasant-hearted people of the Rhine" that he asserted, in October 1914, that "the Kaiser and his military machine must be whipped back into Prussia." Indeed, during the initial months of the war he entertained the opinion that the conflict would not only liberate the people of Germany but would further "the progress of industrial and true liberty in all the nations." "I do not believe a devastating war in Europe will stop the labor struggle," Eastman wrote. "I believe it will hasten the days of its triumph."[12]

Eastman's optimism about the war's "liberating" effects was dispelled during a two months' visit to Europe in the summer of 1915. The experience of witnessing the conflict firsthand led him to see "only a dreariness of horror" in the war. In an article written shortly after his return, he stated: "This war has no more sport in it than it has dramatic action. It is merely a routine businesslike killing and salting down of the younger men of each country involved—twenty thousand a day, perhaps, all told." Although he continued to call for a German defeat ("I earnestly desire to see the Kaiser fail of victory"), he was sufficiently sobered by the sight of "mangled bodies" that he changed the banner of his editorial column in the *Masses* from "Knowledge and Revolution" to "Revolutionary Progress," as if to indicate by the milder slogan approval of "any measure which narrows the gulf between the owning and working class." The realities of armed conflict had made him cautious about the advocacy of violence, more concerned with keeping America out of the war than with proletarian revolutionism.[13]

Following Eastman's return from Europe, the *Masses* took on an increasingly antiwar tone, becoming in its editor's words, "a kind of spearhead for the native American resistance to our intervention in the European war." The popular monthly denounced "bloodthirsty ministers," "war-mongering Christians," and "unscrupulous patriots" such as Theodore Roosevelt and Elihu Root; urged Congress to stand firm against those who would push the nation into war; and ran graphically anti-militarist cartoons by Robert Minor, Boardman Robinson, and Art Young. As Eastman recalled years later: "It seemed to me that all I loved in my country, all that I thought of as 'American' would be lost if the spirit of militarism got a foothold on these shores. I was fighting off an invader—giving no quarter, taking no prisoners." The only "war" he favored was that against the advocates of military preparedness. And in that struggle he was willing to return blow for blow. When Roosevelt denounced American pacifists as "mollycoddles and college sissies," Eastman declared his readiness "to walk up and smash him."[14]

Beginning in the spring of 1916, Eastman enthusiastically supported the American Union Against Militarism, which his sister, Crystal, helped organize in an effort "to stop the war in Europe, to organize the world for peace at the close of the war, and to guard democracy . . . against the subtle dangers of militarism." Under the auspices of this organization, the *Masses'* editor mounted the speaker's platform on numerous occasions to exhort audiences to insist on American neutrality; testified before the Military Committee of the United States Senate in opposition to a bill calling for compulsory military training; and, in March 1917, joined Randolph Bourne and Amos Pinchot in demanding a popular referendum on America's entry into the war.[15]

Moreover, independently of the American Union Against Militarism, but in cooperation with his sister and several other members of that organization, he took part in a last-minute effort to stop the war with paid advertising. Triple-column fourteen-point manifestoes urging the public to petition President Wilson and the Congress "to use every expedient of diplomacy and economic pressure to bring the belligerents into conference" were published in the newspapers of Chicago, New York, and many other cities.

In the aftermath of American intervention, Eastman adopted a stand aptly characterized by historian William L. O'Neill as "total resistance to total war." His contributions to the *Masses* flamed with rebellion: he supported the Socialist Party's St. Louis Proclamation, denounced those Socialists who defected, denied Wilson was waging a "war for democracy," attacked conscription, and called for immediate peace. So adamant was he in opposing the draft that he followed an appeal to all those "who love liberty and democracy" to "resist conscription" with the personal declaration: "I do not recognize the right of a government to draft me to a war whose purposes I do not believe in. But to draft me to a war whose purposes it will not so much as communicate to my ear, seems an act of tyranny, discordant with the memory even of the decent kings."[16]

When asked in August 1917 to tour the country on behalf of the People's Council of America for Democracy and the Terms of Peace, Eastman saw no alternative but to accept: "It was a challenge to back up all the things I had been saying in the *Masses.* . . . I had to deliver the goods . . . I had to go. There was no way out. . . ." Accordingly, he embarked on a speaking tour which took him to cities ranging in size from Detroit, Michigan, to Parkston, South Dakota. For the most part, his remarks against the war were either warmly applauded or quietly tolerated. But in Fargo, North Dakota, he encountered sufficient hostility to cause him to cut short his speech and depart the city in haste. As he confessed in recalling the Fargo experience years later, "Fear had won out . . . over pride. . . . I was faint. I was chilly, I was sick."[17]

Eastman's tour coincided with a government campaign to suppress the *Masses.* Postmaster General Albert S. Burleson, an administration spokesman empowered by the Espionage and Sedition Acts to deny newspapers and political journals their second-class mailing privileges if they contained material considered to be in violation of the law, ordered New York City Postmaster T. G. Patten to exclude the August 1917 issue from the mails. Moreover, the September and later issues were also denied the second-class mailing privilege, even if wholly free of objectionable passages, on the ground that since the August number had not been mailed the *Masses* was an irregular publication and therefore not "a newspaper or periodical within the meaning of the law." As a consequence, at the end of 1917, following the release of the combined November-December issue, the magazine ceased publication. There was no other choice. Exclusion from the mails meant that newsstands were the only mean by which the *Masses* could be circulated. And the journal had not only been removed from the subway and elevated newsstand of New York, but had also been banned by the large magazine distributing companies of Boston and Philadelphia. Burleson's view of the *Masses'* editor as a "traitor" and of its antiwar message as "rank treason" was widely shared. The suppression of the magazine may indeed have been what the *New York Call* dubbed a display of "high-handed tyranny," but to many Americans it was a commendable act of patriotism.[18]

For Eastman, the tragedy of the *Masses'* untimely end was heightened by the attitude of Woodrow Wilson, with whom he had enjoyed friendly relations since 1912, when the two men had met at a banquet in Syracuse, New York, and discussed women's suffrage. In a declaration released to the press at the

end of September 1917, the President responded negatively to
a letter from Eastman asking if the government's treatment of
the *Masses* was not an unwarranted violation of freedom of the
press. "I think that a time of war must be regarded as wholly
exceptional," Wilson asserted. "It is legitimate to regard things
which would in ordinary circumstances be innocent as very dangerous to the public welfare. . . ." What Eastman viewed as "an
impractical way to conduct a war for democracy," Wilson considered a necessity: "I can only say that line must be drawn and
that we are trying. . . ."[19]

Even more disheartening to Eastman, in November he and
six other persons associated with the *Masses* were indicted by
a federal grand jury in New York City on the charge of having
violated the Espionage Act by conspiring to cause "insubordination, disloyalty, mutiny, and refusal of duty in the military and
naval forces of the United States." Eastman, who was regarded
as the leader and instigator of the group, was charged for his
article "A Question," one of the "objectionable" pieces that had
helped prompt the suppression of the August issue. Essentially,
it was an expression of admiration for the courage of those who
resisted conscription on moral grounds. Other materials cited in
the indictment included articles by John Reed and Floyd Dell,
cartoons by Art Young and Henry J. Glintenkamp, and a poem
by Josephine Bell. C. Merrill Rogers, Jr., the magazine's business
manager, was charged with having "unlawfully, willfully, know-
ingly and feloniously" attempted to use the mails for the trans-
mission of matters declared to be unmailable.[20]

The ensuing trial—described by defendant Floyd Dell as "like
a scene from Alice in Wonderland rewritten by Dostoevsky"—
took place in New York City during the latter half of April
1918, when the newly founded *Liberator* was already in its second
number. Since Glintenkamp simply failed to show up (having,
in Eastman's words, "waded the Rio Grande and joined the
'Soviet of Slackers' in Mexico") and Reed learned of the indictment too late to return from Russia, where he had gone the
previous August, only five of the seven defendants were in
court; and of the five only four were actually tried. On the motion of chief counsel Morris Hillquit, the judge dismissed the
indictment against Josephine Bell on the grounds that her poem

"A Tribute" had been her only contribution to the *Masses* and
that, since the other defendants had met her for the first time when
she appeared in court, she could hardly be accused of conspiracy.
One cannot avoid making the observation that the judge might
just as easily have released Bell on the ground that her piece
of super-free verse was utterly innocuous:

> Emma Goldman and Alexander Berkman
>   Are in prison tonight,
> Although the night is tremblingly beautiful
> And the sound of water climbs down the rocks
> And the breath of night air moves through
>   the multitudes and multitudes of leaves
> That love to waste themselves for the sake
>   of the summer.
> Emma Goldman and Alexander Berkman
>   Are in prison tonight,
> But they have made themselves elemental forces
> Like the water that climbs down the rocks;
> Like the wind in the leaves;
> Like the gentle night that holds us;
> They are working on our destinies;
> They are forging the love of nations. . . .[21]

Eastman's testimony, extending over a period of nearly three
days, revealed that his view of the war had altered during the
months between the November indictment and the trial. Althoug
he reaffirmed his distaste for the "ritual of patriotism" and
spoke out strongly in defense of both freedom of the press and
the right of conscientious objection to war, he announced on
April 22 that he had come around to the belief that "this is a
war for liberty and freedom." It was not that he now favored
the war; on the contrary, he continued to regard it as a tragic
mistake. But, convinced by the harsh terms of the Treaty of
Brest-Litovsk that Germany intended to crush Soviet Russia,
and favorably impressed by the seeming sympathy and considera
tion for the Bolsheviks offered in President Wilson's Fourteen
Points, he had arrived at the conclusion that only an Allied victory would bring about the type of peace he desired: "a peace
without forcible annexations, without punitive indemnities,
with free development and self-determination for all peoples."[22]

By the time of the second *Masses* trial, five months later, it was no longer possible to equate Wilson's diplomacy with the foreign policy of the Bolsheviks. With the war nearing an end, Lenin's regime was not threatened by Germany, as had been the case in April, but by the United States, which had sent troops into Siberia. As a consequence of these changed circumstances, and also because the government seemed to have assumed an even tougher attitude toward opponents of the war, Eastman was far more critical of the administration than he had been at the first trial. His three-hour address to the jury on October 4 included an endorsement of the Socialist Party's St. Louis Proclamation condemning America's entrance into the war, an emphatic denial of the charge that the defendants had conspired to defy the military laws of the nation, and the accusation that the government was "violating not only the principles of the United States Constitution, but the spirit and principles of free government as they existed on the earth from the beginning."

The trial's outcome spared Eastman the challenge of having to prove the accuracy of his courtroom assertion: "I am not afraid to spend the better part of my life in a penitentiary, if my principles have brought me to it." As in the first trial, the jury was unable to agree on a verdict. Moreover, that eight jurors voted for acquittal convinced the authorities that further prosecution would be useless. On 10 January 1919 the indictment against the *Masses* defendants was dismissed. Whether or not the results would have been the same had the accused been poor and foreign-born is open to conjecture. Eastman, Reed, Dell, and Young shared the opinion that their "old American lineage" was a decided advantage. One suspects, however, that the determinative factor in the ordeal's outcome was the obvious weakness of the government's case. By any objective standard of judgment, the prosecution failed to prove violation of the Espionage Act.[23]

The final episode in the drama of Eastman's opposition to the war occurred shortly after the trial. On October 15 he received a notice from his draft board informing him that he had been placed in Class I and ordering him to appear for a physical examination on November 2. "Failure to do so," the notice warned, "is a misdemeanor punishable by one year in prison . . .

or immediate induction into military service." Consistent with
the anticonscription stand he had taken in the columns of the
Masses, he wrote to the board: "I do not recognize the right of
a government to conscript the bodies of its citizens for service
upon a foreign soil. I think it is an abandonment of those principles of human liberty upon which the American republic was
founded. In the name of those principles, therefore, I must
decline to serve." To Eastman's good fortune, he was reclassified
in time to avoid a confrontation with the government. Hence,
while Debs and other antiwar dissidents languished in prison,
Eastman remained untrammeled in the pursuit of what he
labeled "the old utopian goal of all social rebels, a 'Society of
the Free and Equal.' "[24]

CHAPTER FOUR

JOHN REED

(1887–1920)

REVOLUTIONARY JOURNALIST

This patriotism, what a humanly fine, stupid instinct gives birth to it, the sacrifice for an ideal, the
self-immolation for something greater than self. Generation after generation surging up to the guns to be
shot to death for an ideal so extremely vague that
they never know what they are fighting for. . . .

—From John Reed's unpublished typescript
"Rule Britannia!," 1914.

To the official Americans in Petrograd, as to most
Americans at home, he was provocative, inconsider-
ate, intolerant, needlessly offensive. His picture of
life was fragmentary in the extreme. He could be
grievously wrong about many things (though seldom
about those he saw with his own eyes). His critical
attitude toward his own country and its society had
in it all the irritating brashness of ignorant and dis-
respectful youth, with no redeeming modesty, no
seemly respect for age and experience. He bore his
antagonism to his own society at the worst possible
time: when the feelings of Americans about their
own country had been aroused to a white heat of
intensity, when their own capacity for tolerance was
least.

—George F. Kennan on John Reed, 1958.

When the Bolsheviks seized power in Russia at the beginning of November 1917, they were enthusiastically observed by a young American radical who subsequently reported his impressions in a book still considered the best eyewitness account of the revolution, *Ten Days That Shook the World* (1919). The American was Max Eastman's proudly unpatriotic friend and *Masses'* colleague John Reed, "a combination of explosive vitality and sustained immaturity," who may very well have been one of the most talented journalists of his generation. An official in the first Soviet government and its first American "martyr," he is remembered by some as "an inveterate traitor . . . always taking the side of murderers, liars and cheats" and by others as an adventurer who sought "to organize his experience into something that had meaning and stature."[1]

Born in Portland, Oregon, the son of Charles J. Reed—a prosperous Roosevelt liberal who had once served as a United States marshal—John attended a fashionable preparatory school in Morristown, New Jersey, before entering Harvard in 1906. During his university years, he became president of the Cosmopolitan Club, served on the editorial boards of the *Lampoon* and the *Monthly,* and was made ivy orator and poet. In 1911, the year following his graduation, he joined the staff of the *American Magazine,* and in 1912, published "Sangar," a piece of allegory, romanticism, and brotherly love, considered by many his best verse.

Under the tutelage of his father's old friend Lincoln Steffens, the famous muckraking journalist and reformer, Reed soon turned to political issues of the day and became an active spokesman for social reform. In 1913 he joined the staff of the *Masses* and from then on took part in various manifestations protesting exploitation of labor. The first of his many arrests occurred in Paterson, New Jersey, in 1913 for supporting the strikers in the silk mills. Shortly after his release he staged the massive "Pageant of the Paterson Strike" in Madison Square Garden for the benefit of the strikers.

Late in 1913 the *Metropolitan* sent Reed to Mexico, where for four months he was a correspondent with Pancho Villa's revolutionary army. His brilliant, if biased, interviews and color-photo stories of the revolution, later republished in book form as *Insurgent Mexico* (1914), brought him a national reputation as a war correspondent. Walter Lippmann, who had been a classmate of his at Harvard, was sufficiently impressed by the effort to remark that "with Jack Reed reporting begins." Yet Lippmann went on to temper his praise with some well deserved criticism of Reed's lack of detachment: "Wherever his sympathies marched with the facts, Reed was superb. . . . But where his feelings conflicted with the facts, his vision flickered."

The journalistic bias noted by Lippmann was obvious in Reed's coverage of the First World War—a conflict he condemned even before observing it as a corresondent for the *Metropolitan.* Just before departing for Europe in 1914, he expressed himself in a bluntly worded article in the *Masses.* "The real war, of which this sudden outburst of death and destruction is only an incident, began long ago," he wrote. "It has been raging for tens of years, but its battles have been so little advertised that they have been hardly noted. It is a clash of traders. . . . We must not be duped by this editorial buncombe about Liberalism going forth to Holy War against Tyranny. This is not Our War."[2]

Reed saw little with which to identify himself on either side of the belligerents. Although he tended to view Germany as the "underdog," declaring that the war had broken out primarily as a result of the determination of France and Great Britain to maintain their own colonial systems in Africa and Asia while preventing the expansion of Imperial Germany, he was bitterly critical of the "crack-brained bombast of the Kaiser" and "the hideous Gospel of Blood and Iron." And he was still harsher in denouncing the "hypocrisy" of England, "a nation that has crushed more human liberty and drenched the world with more rivers of blood than any other." How dare this "bully of the world . . . pose as the champion of the virtue of the human race!," he exclaimed in an article the *Metropolitan* judiciously refused to print. Let no one be deceived by the "lies and distortions" of the British press into believing that England is fighting a "Democratic War." Liberal England has been converted "in an instant . . . into a perfect despotism."[3]

Reed's tour of duty as a European war corresondent was terribly depressing for him. "I have come to hate Europe," he wrote his mother.[4] In none of the countries visited did he encounter the idealism and spontaneity which had stirred him in the Mexican revolution. The whole affair seemed dull and gloomy, a vast, irreducible stalemate in which the people on both sides were docile and indifferent. Paris, London, Berlin—everywhere he traveled—he found the same story: Parisians were "tranquil, ignorant, apathetic"; the British obeyed of their own free will, fighting "because their fathers fought before them"; and the German people, "corrupted and coerced, . . . went to war almost without a protest." For Reed the lesson was clear: "Military service plants in your blood the germ of blind obedience, . . . it produces one class of Commanders in your state and your industries, and accustoms you to do what they tell you even in time of peace." Let others "live half-frozen in a trench," up to their waists in water, he declared.

I hate soldiers. I hate to see a man with a bayonet fixed on his rifle, who can order me off the street. I hate to belong to an organization that is proud of obeying a caste of superior beings, that is proud of killing free ideas, so that it may the more efficiently kill human beings in cold blood. . . I, for one, refuse to join.[5]

The *Metropolitan's* outspoken correspondent may—as Julian Street later alleged in the *Saturday Evening Post*—have had "a love of weapons and of military games" as a child, but he had no intention of risking the horrible wounds he had observed while visiting a German military hospital.[6]

Ironically, neither Reed's scorn of soldiering nor his memory of the hospitalized German whose stomach was so damaged by a shell that "nourishment would have to be injected into his wrist with a hypodermic syringe all his life" prevented him from a foolhardy action that resulted in considerable embarrassment. During a night under fire in a German trench in occupied France, he accepted an officer's invitation to fire a Mauser in the direction of the French lines. The escapade, indiscreetly reported to the *New York Post* by fellow-correspondent Robert Dunn, not only made Reed the butt of abusive editorials in the pro-Allied newspapers, but caused him to be barred from France.[7]

Reed returned to New York in January 1915, but stayed only briefly. In early spring the *Metropolitan* sent him off to cover the war in Eastern Europe where he remained until October.

Accompanied by Boardman Robinson, an English-born artist whose cartoons frequently appeared in the *Masses,* he worked his way from Italy up through the Balkans into Russia and then circled back through Turkey, Bulgaria, and Serbia. His experiences were, if anything, even more depressing than those of his trip in the west. As he recounted in his reports to the *Metropolitan,* republished in 1916 as *The War in Eastern Europe,* he felt himself completely surrounded by death and disease. In Serbia, a devastated and typhus-ridden land he dubbed "The Country of Death," "battlefields, villages, and roads stank with the lightly buried dead, and the streams were polluted with the bodies of men and horses." The ground between the trenches in Goutchevo, Reed would later recall in an article written for the *New York World,* was so filled with "rotting dead" that his "feet sank into awful masses of putrefaction, crawling with maggots. . . .Occasionally a withered hand or foot with bits of cloth clinging to it stuck grotesquely from the ground." Yet it was not such frightful carnage alone that revolted him. He was equally sickened by the widespread corruption in officialdom. It seemed to him that virtually half the officials of Eastern Europe were taking advantage of the war to line their pockets with graft.

Back in New York in early 1916, Reed expressed increasing alarm at America's drift toward war. Speaking at the Labor Forum, he combined a vivid description of the horrors he had observed in Europe with an emphatic denunciation of the "militaristic propaganda" issuing from Theodore Roosevelt and other adovcates of "preparedness." Before the Columbia University Social Study Club he warned that warfare does not disgust men with killing, but gives them a taste for it. Before the Intercollegiate Socialist Society he announced that a "drilled nation in the power of the capitalist classes is dangerous, but a drilled nation in the power of the workers would be mighty interesting." The development of "unofficial armies" controlled by workers willing to "familiarize themselves with guns" and "to train just a little now and then" would not only provide the nation a defense against foreign invasion, but might result in "more attention and respect" being given to labor's demands for better conditions.[8]

Reed's most vehement attack on those who were urging that

the nation make ready for war came in the wake of a massive "preparedness" parade in New York. In a *Masses* article of July 1916, titled "At the Throat of the Republic," he declared that the enemy was not Germany and her allies. The enemy was "that 2% of the people of the United States who own 60% of the national wealth, that band of unscrupulous 'patriots' who have already robbed him [the workingman] of all he has, and are now planning to make a soldier out of him to defend their loot." Chief among those "flooding the country with panic-breeding lies in the campaign for an enormous Army and Navy," he charged, were persons who stood to profit from war production. Both the creator of the National Security League and the majority of the men listed as "founders" of the Navy League were "connected with concerns and establishments which . . . monopolize the manufacture of war-munitions in the United States."

That Reed's chief source of income, the *Metropolitan,* was chagrined by his views is understandable. The selection of Theodore Roosevelt as a contributing editor in February 1915 was symptomatic of the magazine's change in attitude since the beginning of the war. It had moved steadily away from a Socialist position and toward a pro-Allied stance far removed from the antiwar attitude of the young correspondent it had once compared with Stephen Crane and Richard Harding Davis. Yet, in recognition of his talent as a journalist (and perhaps also in the hope that he would "come to his senses"), Reed was kept on the *Metropolitan*'s payroll until shortly after the United States broke off relations with Germany. Even then, he was not fired outright but was given to understand that his work would not be accepted until he reflected the viewpoint of the editors.[9]

Although Reed was by no means an ardent Wilsonian, his preoccupation with keeping the United States out of the war prompted him to endorse the President for a second term in 1916. With Helen Keller, John Dewey, and others he signed an appeal to Socialists to vote for Wilson because "he has kept us out of war. . . . Every radical's vote cast for Benson helps Hughes. Every 'protest' vote is a luxury dearly bought." When George Creel, chairman of the Committee on Public Information, organized a group of fifty writers to reelect the President, Reed joined that too, signing a widely circulated statement to the effect that under Wilson "international law has been upheld, humanity and civilization served, and the horror of a world war averted." Wilson's "only real principles" are "few enough," Reed conceded in a letter to the Socialist Party's National Executive Committee, but they "are on our side."[10]

When the Wilson administration broke off diplomatic relations with Germany early in 1917, Reed felt deceived and betrayed. Ignoring the counsel of Lincoln Steffens and other friends that he should restrain himself, that it was "undemocratic" to continue to rail against a conflict that had become "inevitable," he announced in the *Masses* and the *New York Call:*

> I know what war means. I have been with the armies of all the belligerents except one, and I have seen men die, and go mad, and be in hospitals suffering hell; but there is a worse thing than that. War means an ugly mob-madness, crucifying the truth-tellers, choking the artists, side-tracking reforms, revolutions, and the working of social forces. Already those in America who oppose the entrance of their country into the European melée are called "traitors," and those who protest against the curtailing of our meagre rights of free speech are spoken of as "dangerous lunatics."
>
> ... Whose war is this? Not mine. I know that hundreds of thousands of American workingmen employed by our great financial "patriots" are not paid a living wage. I have seen poor men sent to jail for long terms without a trial, and even without any charge. Peaceful strikers, and their wives and children, have been shot to death, burned to death, by private detectives and militia men. The rich have steadily become richer, and the cost of living higher, and the workers proportionally poorer. These toilers don't want war—not even civil war. But the speculators, the employers, the plutocracy—they want it, just as they did in Germany and in England; and with lies and sophistries they will whip up our blood until we are savage—and then we'll fight and die for them.
>
> ... Those of us who voted for Woodrow Wilson did so because we felt his mind and his eyes were open, because he had kept us out of the mad-dog fight of Europe, and because the plutocracy opposed him. ... The President didn't ask us; he won't ask us if we want war or not. The fault is not ours. It is not our war.[11]

In April, when the "inevitable" occurred, Reed made clear at once that he had no intention of following his country. At an antiwar rally in Washington on the evening that President Wilson requested a joint session of Congress to declare war on Germany, he mounted the platform and exclaimed, "This is not my war, and

I will have nothing to do with it!" Ten days later, appearing at the hearing of the House Judiciary Committee on the Espionage Bill, he complained that if the measure was passed, it would "destroy democratic institutions." And on April 14, at a hearing on the Conscription Bill, he maintained: "I am not a peace-at-any-price man, or a thorough pacifist, but I would not serve in this war. . . . I have no personal objection to fighting. I just think that the war is unjust on both sides, that Europe is mad, and that we should keep out of it."[12]

That Congress should compound the error of intervening in Europe by introducing conscription was to Reed unthinkable, and he underscored his testimony by publishing in the *New York Call* of April 19 an open letter to the members of Congress titled "Why I Am Against Conscription." "Conscription will . . . forcibly drive into the trenches boys of unformed minds, boys too young . . . to decide the awful questions of life and death and international ethics," he insisted. "Conscription is undemocratic and un-American." It "not only drills men's bodies but their minds. It makes them obedient to authority, whether right or wrong, . . . and gives them a hatred of independent thought and contempt for human life. . . . Men who have had their militar training carry the belligerent impulses and the blind respect for authority back into their homes, until the whole nation is permeated with it."

Reed's anguish over the enactment of the Selective Service Bill in May 1917 was made all the more acute by the affect that his opposition to the war was having on his personal affairs. The pages of the *Metropolitan* were closed to him; he was shunned by persons once counted as friends; he was bombarded by letters from his family in Portland begging him to cease his shameful activities; and—as if to add insult to injury—he was attacked for his status as a feature writer for the *New York Mail,* a publication which he learned only belatedly was subsidized by the German government. Small wonder that the autobiographical essay which he wrote just a few months before his thirtieth birthday was permeated with self-doubt and despondency:

I am twenty-nine years old, and I know that this is the end part of my life, the end of youth. . . . I must find myself again. Some men seem to get their direction early. . . . I have no idea what I shall be or do one month from now. Whenever I have tried to become some one thing, I have failed . . . only by drifting with the wind have I found myself. . . . I wish with all my heart that the proletariat would rise and take their rights. . . . But I am not sure any more that the working class is capable of revolution, peaceful or otherwise. The War has been a terrible shatterer of faith in economic and political idealism, . . . a stoppage of the life and ferment of human evolution. I am waiting, waiting for it all to end, for life to resume so I can find my work.[13]

Little occurred to improve Reed's mood during the ensuing summer. Indeed, the period from June to mid-August was perhaps the emptiest and dreariest which he had ever endured. Although he continued to speak out against the war and the "judicial tyranny" reflected in the arrest of Emma Goldman and Alexander Berkman on charges of conspiring to obstruct the draft, he was dissatisfied with his work, disillusioned with many of his former associates, and discontented with the world in general.[14] Feeling very much the lonely and abused prophet, he seemed to take an almost macabre delight in predicting the national suffering to come. " 'Cheero the war spirit' . . . won't last long," he wrote in the *New York Mail*. "Our streets will slowly fill with pale figures in uniform, leaning on Red Cross nurses; with men who have arms off, hands off, faces shot away, men hobbling on crutches, pieces of men. Then New York will not laugh anymore. Europe has stopped laughing long ago."[15]

Such was Reed's attitude when, on 17 August 1917, having been exempted from the draft because of a kidney operation,* he set sail for Russia as a correspondent for the *Masses* and the *New York Call.* The last article he wrote before departing—his first, and only, contribution to the magazine *Seven Arts*—expressed what he felt most deeply about America's participation in the war: "This is not a popular war, and . . . we are not going democratically about 'making the world safe for democracy.' "
Thus, it came as no surprise to Reed that many of the foreigners accompanying him aboard the Danish steamer *United States* were of the opinion "that the United States had a magnificient opportunity to play peace-maker to the exhausted world, and

---

*Reed's left kidney was removed at Johns Hopkins Hospital in Baltimore, Maryland, on 22 November 1916.

lost; and that we have interminably lengthened the war by coming in; and that the conventional fire of libertarian ideals has passed from America's hands into those of Russia."

The hostility directed against Reed as a result of such antiwar pronouncements was further increased by reports of his conduct in Russia. Instead of merely praising the Bolshevik coup d'état the controversial correspondent plunged enthusiastically into revolutionary activities which the American Embassy in Petrograd considered highly inappropriate. Among other things, he wrote much of the Bolshevik propaganda dropped over the German lines, publicly announced a desire to help free the "oppressed and exploited masses" of the United States, and—shortly before departing for home—accepted appointment as Soviet consul in New York. Although none of these actions provoked the authorities in Washington to issue a charge of "treason," they did cause considerable irritation—particularly in the offices of the State Department, which responded immediately to word of Reed's consulship with the announcement that the appointment would not be recognized, that Reed would have no standing.[16]

Reed arrived back in New York on 28 April 1918. He had attempted to hasten his return in order to appear at the trial of the *Masses* editors, with whom he had been indicted under the Espionage Act for his article "Knit a Strait-Jacket for Your Soldier Boy."* But he was too late; the trial had ended in a hung jury just one day before his ship docked. Since the charge of conspiracy to obstruct the draft still stood, however, he was informed that he would have to report at the Federal Building on April 29. In the meantime, he was held on board ship for more than eight hours while federal agents searched his belongings for Bolshevik propaganda. The agents confiscated his papers, including the notes for *Ten Days That Shook the World,* but they were later returned to him.[17]

Seemingly unintimidated by the possibility that the second *Masses* trial might result in his imprisonment, Reed spent most of his time during the next five months "making America Bol-

---

*The article had appeared in the suppressed August 1917 issue of the *Masses.* It consisted solely of excerpts from a newspaper report concerning the large incidence of mental illness among servicemen. Reed was responsible only for the title.

shevik-conscious." He spoke at numerous meetings in the East and across the Middle West, steadfastly supporting the merits of Bolshevism; he accepted an assignment from the *Liberator* to cover the Chicago trial of William D. Haywood and ninety-nine other members of the I. W. W.; and on two separate occasions he succeeded in provoking the authorities into arresting and charging him with sedition—both times for an "incendiary speech," the first in Philadelphia and the second in New York.*

Reed's testimony at the second *Masses* trial, although hardly "incendiary," dispelled any doubt remaining as to either his hatred of the war or his commitment to the class struggle. Called to the stand on 3 October 1918, he freely admitted that he was opposed to the war, that he was a Socialist, and that he believed in a revolution of the proletariat against the capitalists. He was less than candid on only one point. When asked by Judge Manton if he had opposed military recruitment, he responded negatively.[18]

The remaining two years of Reed's life were anticlimactic. In September 1919, shortly after taking a leading part in the formation of the Communist Labor Party, he returned to Russia, where he participated in the Second Congress of the Communist International and served as a member of its Executive Committee. In the fall of 1920, while attending the Congress of Oriental Nationalities at Baku, he ate some unwashed fruit, caught typhus, and died on October 17—just five days before his thirty-third birthday. Befitting his status as the author of what Lenin considered to be the best book on the Bolshevik seizure of power, Reed was buried in Moscow's Red Square, beneath the Kremlin Wall.

It is difficult to quarrel with historian John P. Diggins's assertion that John Reed—like his friend Max Eastman—offered no inspiring legacy to future generations of American radicals. Yet, considering the record of his opposition to the First World War, it is hardly justifiable to dismiss him as "the poet-playboy of the Lyrical Left." A dedicated revolutionary whose journalistic endeavors reflected a blazing honest and a purity of idealism, he lived a life seldom equaled in creative energy and enthusiasm for the transformation of society. In the final analysis, one is tempted

---

*The government dropped its case against him for his speech in New York shortly before the second *Masses* trial. He was acquitted of the Philadelphia charges in 1919.

to agree with George F. Kennan that Reed's immature opinions and provocative behavior "would have been better met by an amused sympathy than by criminal indictments."[19]

CHAPTER FIVE

EMMA GOLDMAN

(1869–1940)

ANARCHIST PACIFIST

Come! Let us lay a crazy lance in rest,
And tilt at windmills under a wild sky.
For who would die so petty and unblest
That dare not tilt at something ere he die,
Rather than, screened by safe majority,
Preserve his little life to little ends
And never raise a rebel battle-cry.

—From a poem sent to Emma Goldman
by John Galsworthy in 1934.

Once called "Red Emma" and "the mother of anarchy in
America," Emma Goldman was among the most active and auda-
cious rebels of her time. A woman of enormous courage, who
both preached and practiced the philosophy of freedom, she
provoked extremes of adulation and criticism. Eugene Debs
described her as "one of the sincerest women" he knew, and
the *Nation* asserted in 1922 that her name should be on any list
of the twelve greatest living American women. By way of contrast, J. Edgar Hoover, denounced her as one of the "most dangerous radicals in this country," and an angry mob in San Diego,
California, once threatened to "strip her naked" and "tear out
her guts."[1]

Born in Kovno, Russia (Kaunas in modern Lithuania), the
daughter of a government theater manager, Goldman emigrated
to the United States in 1886 and worked for a time in a clothing

factory in Rochester, New York. By 1889 she had espoused anarchism and had moved to New York City where she became associated with the emigré Russian revolutionist Alexander Berkman and with Johann Most, editor of the German-language anarchist paper *Freiheit.* During the next several decades, she took part in strikes, practiced free love, waged numerous fights for free speech, ran the anarchist literary and political monthly *Mother Earth,* toured the country lecturing on subjects ranging from Ibsen to birth control to the evils of patriotism, and was several times imprisoned (once for urging women to "keep their minds open and their wombs closed").[2]

With the outbreak of the First World War, Goldman attacked the preparedness program of the Wilson administration. Following American entry, she and Berkman organized an anticonscription campaign, which led to their arrest in June 1917 on charges of conspiracy to obstruct the operation of the selective service law. They were convicted and sentenced to two years' imprisonment. In 1919, shortly after her release from the Missouri state penitentiary in Jefferson City, Goldman was deported to Russia.

Although she headed for Russia with great enthusiasm, believing the Soviet experiment to be the symbol of "humanity's hope," she was soon disillusioned, proving herself an opponent not only of rationalized conformity in the United States but also of rationalized terror in Russia. "It remains true, as it has through all progress," Emma wrote after expatriating herself from Russia, "that only the libertarian spirit and method can bring man a step further in his eternal striving for the better, finer, and freer life. . . . The authoritarian method has been a failure all through history and now it has again failed in the Russian Revolution."[3] Her book *My Disillusionment in Russia* (1925) remains the best analysis by an anarchist of the failure of the Russian Revolution.

After leaving Russia, Goldman lived for brief periods in England, France (where she wrote her vigorous autobiography *Living My Life* [1931]), Spain, and Canada, visiting the United States only once—in 1934—when she received permission to return on a ninety-day visa. A staunch defender of the Catalonian revolutionists during the Spanish Civil War, she died in 1940 in Canada where she had gone the year before in a last-minute effort to raise funds for their lost cause.

In a letter written 8 August 1917, just one month after her conviction on charges of conspiracy to obstruct the draft, Emma Goldman informed poet Bayard Boyeson of Athol, Massachusetts, of her belief that she had never in all the twenty-seven years of her public career done "better and more important work" than that against the World War. "I am convinced," she asserted, "that the day will come when all those who at the present moment are ready to lay down their lives in this terrible war will realize that those who stood out against it had prophetic eyes."[4]

Protesting the World War came naturally to Goldman. For many years prior to the outbreak of that great conflict she had campaigned against the evils of militarism, objecting to all war except that waged for the purpose of overthrowing the capitalist system and establishing industrial control for the working class. She regarded the "military spirit" as "the most merciless, heartless and brutal in existence" and placed the responsibility for the legalized murder it engendered squarely on the shoulders of the state, arguing that without governments to lead their subjects to battle, wars would be unthinkable. Governments enable "the predatory rich to make wars to provide foreign markets for the favored ones, with prosperity for the rulers and wholesale death for the ruled." Her remedy for this tragic circumstance was a simple one. The "terrible red streak of war and destruction" would cease when the exploited masses of mankind—mirroring the philosophy of anarchism (which Goldman believed to be "the only theory of a social relationship that values human life above everything else")—told their masters: "Go and do your own killing. We have sacrificed ourselves and our loved ones long enough fighting your battles."[5]

According to Goldman, her hatred of militarism and her "struggle against it" as an "inhuman institution" had begun when, as a child in Russia, she had witnessed young peasants conscripted into the army and torn from their homes and loved ones. However, this allegation is only partly true. While it is quite probable that the "heartbreaking scenes" she had observed during her youth had a decisive effect on her sympathies, Emma refrained from any "struggle" against militarism until, approaching thirty years of age, she agitated against the Spanish-American (1898) and Boer (1899–1902) wars, delivering talks

in the United States, England, and Scotland urging that no one
fight or in any way contribute to the conflicts.[6]

Just as militarism was for Goldman an "inhuman institution,"
its sister doctrine, patriotism, was for her an "insatiable monster"
that "requires allegiance to the flag, which means obedience and
readiness to kill father, mother, brother, sister." Like Leo Tolstoy,
she defined patriotism as a cheap justification for "the training
of wholesale murderers"; emulating Gustave Hervé, she sought
to understand it as "a supersitition artifically created and maintained through a network of lies and falsehoods"; and reminiscent
of Samuel Johnson, she condemned it as "the last resort of
scoundrels." She thus found it especially unfortunate that in
the United States this "pernicious doctrine" was "being inculcated
in the child as something absolute, final, and inalienable." "Children," she wrote in 1908,

are trained in military tactics, the glory of military achievements extolled
in the curriculum, and the youthful minds perverted to suit the government.
Further, the youth of the country is appealed to in glaring posters to join
the army and navy. "A fine chance to see the world!" cries the governmental huckster. Thus innocent boys are morally shanghaied into patriotism,
and the military Moloch strides conquering through the Nation.[7]

Particularly demonstrative of the "evil results" of patriotism,
from Emma's point of view, was the case of a United States
Army private, William Buwalda. In 1908, after fifteen years of
faithful military service, Buwalda was condemned by court-
martial to five years' imprisonment on Alcatraz Island for shaking
Goldman's hand at the conclusion of a lecture she delivered on
patriotism in San Francisco. To the hapless private's command-
ing officer, General Frederick Funston, Buwalda's action was a
"great military offense, infinitely worse than desertion." To
Goldman, on the other hand, Buwalda's "guilt" lay in his naive
belief that "one can be a soldier and exercise his rights as a man
at the same time." She saw the real crime in the "spirit of un-
questioning obedience" that made possible Buwalda's persecution.[8]

For Goldman, who organized and led a committee for the
court-martialed soldier's defense, the affair ended on a triumphant
note. Ten months after his sentencing, Buwalda was pardoned

by President Theodore Roosevelt. Subsequently he joined the anarchist movement.

When war broke out in Europe in 1914, Peter Kropotkin, a Russian geographer and naturalist regarded by many of his contemporaries as the world's leading protagonist of anarchism, sided with the Allied cause and called upon all who cherished the ideals of human progress to help stop the German "invasion" of Western Europe. Although a number of eminent anarchists in Europe endorsed his opinion, Goldman and most other anarchists throughout the world held fast to the antimilitarism and antipatriotism they had so forcefully espoused during times of peace. Regarding the war as a capitalist struggle for power and profit, they believed it ridiculous to favor victory for either side. As these "internationalist" anarchists saw it, their proper task was "to bring about peace on earth and good will towards men"—a goal which Goldman declared could be attained, first, by conceding "the superiority of the individual" over "the organized force known as the state," and, second, by emancipating the masses from the economic and social slavery of capitalism.

Goldman joined her friend and collaborator Alexander Berkman in a spirited campaign against the war during the very month it began, calling in the August 1914 issue of *Mother Earth* for "War on War" ("We proclaim the INSURRECTION AGAINST THE WAR"). And in late October Emma undertook a tour of some two months' duration on which she lectured to audiences in Chicago, Detroit, St. Louis, Cleveland, Pittsburgh, Indianapolis, and several other cities on such topics as "The Psychology of War," "War and Christianity," "Woman and War," and "The Sanctity of Property as a Cause of War."[9]

In both her lectures and her contributions to *Mother Earth* Goldman repeated time and again that capitalism was responsible for the carnage in Europe. As she stated in signing the "International Anarchist Manifesto on the War," published in 1915, "the war . . . is the inevitable and fatal outcome of a society that is founded on the exploitation of the workers, rests on the savage struggle of the classes, and compels Labor to submit to the domination of a minority of parasites who hold both political and economic power." As the war continued to grind on, she began to single out American capitalists as particularly blameworthy. For example, in "The Promoters of the War Mania," written in March 1917, she asserted that "the war would have been at an end long ago, had the American financiers been prevented from investing billions in war loans and had the American munition clique and food speculators not been given the opportunity to supply warring Europe with the means to keep up the slaughter."[10]

Beginning in 1915, another of Goldman's persistent themes became the danger to the United States of "military preparedness," which she believed would lead inevitably to "universal slaughter." In *Mother Earth* and in lectures delivered throughout the country during the spring and summer of 1916 she warned that " 'readiness,' far from assuring peace, has at all times and in all countries been instrumental in precipitating armed conflicts." "[President] Wilson," she maintained, "has but one aim, to serve the big interests, to add to those who are growing phenomenally rich by the manufacture of military supplies." His version of preparedness "will only add to the power of the privileged few and help them to subdue, to enslave and crush Labor." What the workers need is not Wilsonian preparedness, but "industrial and economic preparedness." We "must organize the preparedness of the masses for the overthrow of both capitalism and the state."

Although by early 1917 the signs were unmistakable that the United States was going to be drawn into the contest in Europe, Goldman continued to argue that there was "still time to stem the bloody tide of war, by word of mouth and men and action." American participation in the "European mass-murder" could be prevented if the people would refuse to take part in such folly. "I for one will speak out against war so long as my voice will last, now and during war," she pledged in March. "A thousand times rather would I die, calling to the people of America to refuse to be obedient, to refuse military service, to refuse to murder their brothers, than I should ever give my voice in justification of war, except the one war of all the peoples against their despots and exploiters—the Social Revolution."[11]

As it turned out, of course, there was less time to agitate against American entry than Goldman anticipated. President Wilson asked Congress to declare war on Germany in April and in the following month signed a Draft Bill setting 5 June 1917 as Registration Day for all twenty-one- to thirty-year-old men. America's most famous female anarchist now faced the dilemma of whether or not to uphold her pledge to exhort her countrymen to "refuse to be obedient, to refuse military service, to refuse to murder their brothers."

Goldman and Berkman reacted to the president's advocacy of conscription by arranging a series of protest rallies, by composing a No-Conscription Manifesto of which they distributed 100,000 copies, and by organizing a No-Conscription League with branches in a number of cities. Since, "as a woman and therefore . . . not subject to military service," Goldman felt she could not advise others whether or not to lend themselves as "tool[s] for the business of killing," the League was designed not to urge individuals to refuse service, but rather to agitate against the draft on legal and moral grounds and to support those who chose to resist induction. The League's platform, as summarized in the June 1917 issue of *Mother Earth,* was as follows:

We oppose conscription because we are internationalists, antimilitarists, and opposed to all wars waged by capitalist governments.

We will fight for what we choose to fight for. We will never fight simply because we are ordered to fight.

We believe that the militarization of America is an evil that far outweighs, in its anti-social and anti-libertarian effects, any good that may come from America's participation in the war.

We will resist conscription by every means in our power, and we will sustain those who, for similar reasons, refuse to be conscripted.[12]

The League opened its campaign against conscription on May 18 with a mass protest meeting at New York City's Harlem River Casino. An estimated six thousand persons—including two police stenographers—heard speeches by Goldman, Berkman, Louis Fraina (soon to become a prominent figure in the left wing of the Socialist Party), and a few others. Goldman's address included the charge that the war was being run by Wall Street, a prediction that fifty thousand people in New York City would refuse to register when the conscription census was taken, and a flat denial of the rumor that the meeting was financed by German money.

The next major rally, a huge affair held on June 4 at Hunt's Point Palace in the Bronx, seemed likely to end in violence when a group of soldiers and sailors nearly provoked a riot by throwing light bulbs and threatening to rush the platform. Although several hundred policemen were present, it was Goldman who acted to avoid bloodshed. Hurrying to the speaker's stand, she told the audience that soldiers and sailors had been sent to the rally to make trouble and that the police were in league with them.

If we lose our heads there will be bloodshed, and it will be our blood they will shed! Your presence here and the presence of the multitude outside shouting their approval of every word they can catch, are convincing proof that you do not believe in violence, and it equally proves that you understand that war is the most fiendish violence. War kills deliberately, ruthlessly, and destroys innocent lives. . . . Intelligence and a passionate faith are more convincing than armed police, machine guns, and rowdies in soldiers' coats.

She then succeeded in getting her hearers to file out of the hall in an orderly manner.[13]

Not surprisingly, the Hunt's Point Palace episode did little to improve Goldman's low opinion of soldiers, to whom she referred at a June 11 rally sponsored by the Collegiate League for Peace and Harmony as "scabs who are not worthy of the respect of decent men and women." She might have directed a few harsh words at federal law officers as well had she known what would happen at the end of the meeting. As the audience was dispersing, United States Marshal Thomas D. McCarthy not only arrested a number of men of conscript age who had refused to register, but warned Goldman that she too would be arrested if she organized any more meetings to protest the selective service law.[14]

The last public meeting scheduled by the No-Conscription League was held on June 14 in Forward Hall on New York's Lower East Side. Speaking before a capacity crowd (interspersed with the now customary government stenographers), Goldman embellished her usual remarks against conscription with a denunciation of Judge Julius Mayer, who had the day before sentenced the anarchists Morris Becker and Louis Kramer to maximum terms in the Atlanta Federal Penitentiary for asserting that young men should refuse to register for the draft. At the meeting's close, those men of draft age who could not show a registration card were arrested. As a consequence, Goldman and Berkman, concluding that the authorities intended to use the league's rallies to trap persons who had not registered, resolved to forgo further public gatherings and concentrate instead on written propaganda such as "The Holiday," the introductory article which Emma had contributed to the June issue of *Mother Earth:*

On June 5th [the date on which most young Americans registered for the draft] the Moloch Militarism will sit in pompous state awaiting its victims who are to be dedicated to its gluttonous appetite.

Surrounded by its high dignitaries, courtiers, vassals and lackeys, the monster will reach out for the youth of the land to be sacrificed on the altar of blood and iron, to the glory of God, the servitude of democracy.

Music will drown the groans and curses of the unwilling. Colors will obscure the burning eye of hate. Artificial holiday and merry making will mask the pale tragedy of those whose sons, brothers, lovers and friends are to be offered up for sacrifice on the tear-stained day of June 5th.

In Europe the day of registration for compulsory military service is a day of mourning. Fathers are filled with grim opposition. Mothers rend the air with plaints of despair. Even those who are forced to execute the dictate of their masters, look upon their task as a ghastly duty.

Not so democratic America. To her human tragedy has ever been a cause for rejoicing, whether it be the hanging of Anarchists, the shooting of strikers, the hounding of I. W. W., the lynching of negroes. It is a holiday participated in by a joy-drunk mob gloating over the agony of its victims. So too, on the crucial day of June 5th democratic America will celebrate with song and dance and revelry, to the strains of deafening music and waving of flags, the funeral procession of 500,000 American youths, while the Moloch Militarism sits on his bloody throne ready to devour the sacrifice, yet proclaiming in loud dissonant tones: Praise unto Democracy! Glory unto War![15]

The bitter antimilitarism Goldman was espousing in June 1917 was reflected in her judgment of American Socialists. Those Socialists whom she felt ought to have known better, but had nonetheless come out in favor of President Wilson and intervention (e.g., Upton Sinclair, J. G. Phelps Stokes, and William English Walling), she denounced as "pseudo-revolutionaries" and toadies of "American Kaiserism," identifying them as perfect illustrations of the "black scourge of war in its devastating effect upon the human mind." On the other hand, she defended antiwar

Socialists like Morris Hillquit and Victor Berger whom she had formerly regarded as "prototypes of political conservatism" and "bitter enemies of everything even remotely anarchistic or revolutionary": "We feel constrained to say that the raving against Hillquit and others is sheer madness, and nothing else."[16] Yet Goldman was quite capable of communicating sympathetically with young Americans who supported the war out of a genuine (and, she believed, naive) conviction that what they were doing was in the long-run interests of peace and democracy. Her letter of 8 August 1917 to Bayard Boyesen is a case in point: "I know that you are absolutely sincere in your feeling that by going to fight . . . you will help crush the obvious evils of militarism," she wrote.

> But I am . . . convinced that you will find yourself mistaken. Oh, I know that the general cry is that we have entered the war to make the world safe for Democracy. . . .
> Industrial democracy indeed with negro massacres at home; with the cold blooded lynching of an I. W. W.; with hundreds of Little's* comrades brutally beaten and rushed out of cities; with the burning of men, women and children in Ludlow, Colorad [sic]**; with the suppression of every independent opinion; and the gagging of every brave voice. Really, Bayard, the claim of this country to make the world safe for democracy must make Satan laugh. . . .
> I do not adjudge you a renegade. You are like many others who have been swept off their feet by the cataclysm of war. Perhaps I am a little disappointed because you have always seemed such a sceptic and so very unlike the average cultured American. I had expected that you would see through the net of lies that have been woven for the purpose of blinding people to the real issue, and the real issues my boy are nothing else but profits and conquest.[17]

As noted above, following the protest rally of June 11, federal Marshal Thomas McCarthy had warned that he would arrest Goldman if she organized any more meetings against the draft. On June 15, in response to orders received from Washington, he

---

*Frank Little was the I. W. W.'s most bitter foe of war. He was lynched by Montana vigilantes on 1 August 1917, one week before Goldman's letter to Boyesen.

**The reference here is to the 1914 Ludlow "Massacre," an unprovoked militia attack on striking miners and their families at a Colorado tent camp.

carried out his threat. Goldman and Berkman were arrested in New York City that afternoon and the next morning were arraigned before United States Commissioner Samuel W. Hitchcock on the charge of "conspiracy to induce persons not to register under the Conscription Law." The report of their arrest in the *New York Times* left little doubt of that paper's opinion of the two anarchists' guilt and deserved fate: "Leniency would be out of place. Of their intention and their laborious attempt to stir sedition, to stir treason and rebellion, there is not the slightest doubt. . . ." If convicted, "they should not only be punished by imprisonment but deported to the lands from which they came."

During the several days following the arrest, the radical pair's pacifist attorney, Harry Weinberger, aided by Berkman's companion, M. Eleanor Fitzgerald, worked hard to raise the $25,000 bail set for each of the two defendants. However, by June 21, the day Goldman and Berkman were indicted by a federal grand jury and arraigned before Judge Julius Mayer, only enough money had been contributed by friends and supporters to post bail for Goldman, as a result of which Berkman remained in custody until June 25, two days before the trial began. Not surprisingly, considering the pro-German sentiments commonly attributed to antiwar dissidents at this time, the *New York World* printed a story on June 22 claiming "a report is current that the Kaiser furnished the $25,000 for Emma's release."

When the trial opened in New York City's Federal Building on June 27 (Goldman's forty-eighth birthday), the two defendants were without legal counsel. Against Weinberger's advice, they had decided that the trial would have "meaning" only if they succeeded in turning the courtroom into a forum for the presentation of ideas for which they had long been fighting. Hence, there was no counsel to challenge the selection of the jury—a body which, as finally determined after three days, was decidedly "white collar"—including a jeweler, a perfumer, a real estate dealer, the vice-president of a business firm, two contractors, two salesmen, and a secretary.[18]

The case for the prosecution, as stated by Assistant United States District Attorney Harold A. Content, was based not only on stenographic reports of the May 18–June 14 rallies protesting the draft, but also on copies of *Mother Earth, The Blast,* * and the "No-Conscription Manifesto" seized by McCarthy and his deputies when they arrested Goldman and Berkman on June 15. Content sought to show that the defendants had urged men eligible for the draft not to register; had accepted German funding of their opposition to conscription; had misappropriated money contributed to the No-Conscription League; and had advocated violence at the May 18 rally in the Harlem River Casino.

The charges of "German backing" and the misuse of league funds were both irrelevant and insupportable—and the prosecution wisely spent relatively little time attempting to substantiate them. Far more effort was expended in seeking to establish that the defendants had advocated violence. And on this score Content was for the most part successful. Despite the testimony of nine long-term acquaintances of Goldman that they had never heard her counsel violence, the federal attorney was able to persuade the jury that, regardless of whether she had encouraged violence in her speech of May 18, she did in fact advocate violence.

Ironically, Content offered little evidence in support of the charge on which Goldman and Berkman had been indicted: conspiracy to induce persons not to register. The prosecution relied almost entirely on the testimony of police stenographer William H. Randolph, who maintained that Goldman had asserted in her speech of May 18, "We are going to support the men who will refuse to register and who will refuse to fight." The contention of Goldman and Berkman that they had not urged individuals to avoid registering, but rather had merely offered support to those who refused to be drafted, failed to impress the jurors. Nor were the latter moved in the defendants' favor by Berkman's argument that he and Goldman could hardly have been guilty of conspiracy when they had publicly campaigned against militarism for many years and their position on conscription was known to millions of people.

---

*Edited first by Berkman alone, then by Berkman and Goldman, this radical labor journal was published in San Francisco—and subsequently New York—from 15 January 1916 to 1 June 1917.

Goldman delivered her final address to the jury on July 9, following the summation of the prosecutor and a two-hour speech by Berkman. Since the address indicates clearly that her views on the war had in no way altered since her arrest, and also that she was not at all intimidated by the ordeal of the trial, it merits more than passing consideration.[19]

After ridiculing the "sensational" circumstances under which she and Berkman had been arrested as a "Barnum & Bailey" affair designed to assure that Marshal McCarthy and Assistant District Attorney Content would "go down to posterity and receive immortality," Goldman directed her attention to the charge of conspiracy to induce men of conscription age not to register:

As to the conspiracy: imagine, if you please, people engaged along similar lines for nearly thirty years, always standing out against war. . . , always insisting . . . that all wars are wars among thieves who are too cowardly to fight and who therefore induce the young manhood of the whole world to do the fighting for them—that is our standing; we have proved it by evidence, we have proved it by witnesses, we have proved it by our own position, that always and forever we have stood against war . . . ; imagine also people who for 30 years in succession have stood out against militarism, . . . then say how there can possibly be a conspiracy when people merely continue in their work. . . . What kind of conspiracy is that? . . . I insist that the prosecution has failed utterly, has failed miserably to prove the charge on the indictment of conspiracy. . . .

Moving on to the matter of political violence, Goldman explained to the jurors that, as a "social student" whose business in life it was to ascertain the cause of social evils and difficulties, she had naturally attempted to explain the cause and the reason for acts of individual violence. She had explained "political violence at the bottom" as "the culminating result of organized violence at the top"—"the result of violence which expresses itself in war, which expresses itself in courts, which expresses itself in prisons, which expresses itself in kicking and hounding people for the only crime they are guilty of: of having been born poor." Did the jurors believe that explaining the act of political violence was the same thing as advocating the act? she queried. "If that is your version . . . I say, gentlemen of the jury, you might as well condemn Jesus for having defended the prostitute Mary Magdalen, you might as well say that he advocated prostitution. . . ."

Although Goldman thus denied that she had conspired to persuade people not to register or that she had advocated political violence, she readily admitted to being a conscientious objector:

I am a conscientious objector. What is he? He is impelled . . . by the force of righteous passion for justice, which is the bulwark and mainstay and basis of all our existence and of all our liberty. . . . The conscientious objector . . . does not believe in war, not because he is a coward or a shirker, not because he doesn't want to stand responsible, but because he insists that, belonging to the people whence he has come and to whom he owes life, it is his place to stand on the side of the people, for the people and by the people and not on the side of the governing classes.

In conveying to the jurors her definition of patriotism, Goldman spoke in terms strikingly similar to those of Peter Chaadayev a nineteenth-century Russian aristocrat who maintained that to criticize one's country is to do it a service, to perform an act of love. The kind of patriotism Goldman claimed to represent

is the kind of patriotism which loves America with open eyes. Our relation toward America is the same as the relation of a man who loves a woman, who is enchanted by her beauty and yet who cannot be blind to her defects. And so I wish to state here, in my own behalf and in behalf of hundreds of thousands whom you decry and state to be antipatriotic, that we love America, we love her beauty, we love her riches, we love her mountains and her forests, and above all we love the people who have produced her wealth and riches, who have created all her beauty, we love the dreamers and the philosophers and the thinkers who are giving America liberty. But that must not make us blind to the social faults of America. That cannot make us deaf to the discords in America. That cannot compel us to be inarticulate to the terrible wrongs committed in the name of patriotism and in the name of the country.

Approaching the end of her remarks, Goldman cautioned that whatever the jury's verdict "the tremendous storm brewing in the United States" would not be affected—for the storm was not created by two lone opponents. "That storm was created by the conditions themselves, by the fact that the people before election were promised they would be kept out of war and after election they were dragged into war." Nor, she asserted, would the verdict have more than a temporary affect on her and Berkman:

It will affect us physically; it cannot affect our spirit . . . whether we are found guilty or whether we are placed in jail. . . . Nothing will be changed in our ideas. For even if we were convicted and found guilty and the penalty were, to be placed against a wall and shot dead, I should nevertheless cry out with the great Luther: "Here I am and here I stand and I cannot do otherwise."

Yet, while Goldman was emphatic in maintaining that "nothing on earth" could force her to change her ideas, she made it clear in concluding her hour-long address that she had no wish to be a martyr to the cause of antimilitarism. Asking the jurors to forget that she and Berkman were anarchists, she called upon them to "merely consider the evidence." "Have we been engaged in a conspiracy? Has that conspiracy been proved; have we committed overt acts; have those overt acts been proved? We for the defense say they have not been proved. And therefore your verdict must be not guilty."

Goldman's eloquence was for naught. After deliberating for thirty-nine minutes, the jury declared both defendants guilty. Denying defense motions, first, that "the verdict be set aside as absolutely contrary to the evidence" and, second, that "sentence be deferred for a few days" and "bail be continued at the sum already fixed" in the case, Judge Mayer sentenced each of the defendants to the maximum two years in prison, imposed on them the maximum $10,000 fines, and recommended that they be deported when their sentences were up. Not to be denied the last word, Goldman interrupted the judge's departure from the courtroom with a sarcastic expression of gratitude: "I want to thank you for your leniency and kindness in refusing us a stay of two days, a stay you would have accorded the most heinous criminal. I thank you once more."[20]

It is difficult to avoid the conclusion that the defendants exercised poor judgment in deciding to go into court without an attorney. Yet, considering the circumstances, Goldman can be faulted neither for her parting shot at Mayer nor for subsequently characterizing the trial in her autobiography as a "contest between ideas and organized stupidity."[21] Friends of the defendants were either denied entrance to the proceedings or treated rudely after they gained admittance; the jury was predominantly representative of business or white collar interests; much of the

government's presentation (such as testimony relating to the
defendants' belief in violence—including Content's implication
in his address to the jury that Goldman had asserted in 1901
that President McKinley ought to be shot) was irrelevant to the
crime for which Goldman and Berkman were indicted; Judge
Mayer hardly conveyed an image of impartiality; and, on several
occasions, everyone in the courtroom but the defendants was
compelled to stand when strains of the national anthem permeated the proceedings from a military band playing in the street
outside (those who declined to rise were forcibly removed).

Goldman began serving her sentence at Missouri state prison
in Jefferson City on 6 February 1918, after the United States
Supreme Court found the Draft Act constitutional (January 7)
and affirmed her conviction (January 14).[22] During the period
between the trial and Goldman's incarceration, the government
ruled unmailable *Blast, Mother Earth,* and *Mother Earth Bulletin* (a radical monthly started by Emma and two fellow
anarchists in October 1917). The cover page of Goldman's
pamphlet "Patriotism: A Menace to Liberty" had proved
prophetic. It depicted a woman—helmeted, armored, and bearing a flag labeled "Patriotism"—standing triumphant above a
prostrate female figure draped in a flag bearing the word "Liberty."

At the end of September 1919, shortly after Goldman's release
(she had earned four months off her sentence for good behavior),
a federal court ruled that she had lost her American citizenship, obtained through marriage to one Jacob Kersner in 1887.* Two
months later—under authority of the Alien Act of 16 October
1918, which authorized the government to deport any alien who,
at any time after entering the United States, was found to have
been at the time of entry, or to have become thereafter, a member of an anarchist organization—the Department of Labor
ordered her deported to Russia. Accordingly, on 21 December
1919 she and 248 other radicals left New York aboard the *Bu-
ford,* a vessel the press aptly dubbed the "Soviet Ark." Arriving
in Finland on January 17, Goldman crossed the border into
Russia two days later.

---

*Goldman was married to Kersner, according to Jewish rites, in Rochester, New
York, in February 1887. The couple was divorced less than a year later.

At this writing, Emma Goldman has been dead for well over three decades, and there are doubtless few Americans who remember her as a woman the very mention of whose name caused "palpitation of the heart."[23] Indeed, it is probable that many who are aware of her career and ideas tend to dismiss her as naive and inexcusably idealistic. There is, of course, an element of truth in both judgments. Yet, it would be a mistake to stop there. For, although Goldman was sometimes naive and often idealistic, she was always a courageous and energetic activist. She was impatient; she was hypercritical of those who disagreed with her; she was stubborn and hot-tempered; she was egotistical and cantankerous; and her speeches and writings were not particularly original. But she was also a sincere, warm-hearted, and admirably consistent agitator in behalf of liberty—a woman whose compassion for the oppressed and spirited opposition to economic inequality represented the very best traditions of American radicalism.

CHAPTER SIX

WILLIAM D. HAYWOOD

(1869–1928)

PROLETARIAN ACTIVIST

I love my flag, I do, I do,
Which floats upon the breeze,
I also love my arms and legs,
And neck, and nose and knees.
One little shell might spoil them all
Or give them such a twist,
They would be of no use to me;
    I guess I won't enlist.

I love my country, yes I do
I hope her folks do well,
Without our arms, and legs, and things,
I think we'd look like hell.
Young men with faces half shot off
Are unfit to be kissed,
I've read in books it spoils their looks,
    I guess I won't enlist.

—"I Love My Flag" (author unknown),
Industrial Worker, April 14, 1917.

The leaders of the "Wobblies" (as members of the Industrial Workers of the World were called) were victims of the same circumstances as Emma Goldman when, following America's entry into the war, "subversives" were made to suffer. In August 1918 one hundred members of this revolutionary labor union were convicted of conspiracy to obstruct the government in prosecuting the war and sentenced to prison for terms ranging from one to twenty years. The principal defendant was the union's general secretary-treasurer, William Dudley Haywood, a tall, husky, one-eyed man whom the British Socialist leader J. Ramsay MacDonald had characterized years earlier as "the embodiment of the Sorel philosophy,*. . . a bundle of primitive instincts, a master of direct statement."[1]

Like that of Eugene Debs, the record of "Big Bill" Haywood's early life gives little hint that he would one day be among the best-known radicals in the United States. Born in Salt Lake City, Utah, he grew up with few advantages of wealth or education. He became a hardrock miner at the age of fifteen and worked for many years thereafter in the mines of Nevada, Utah, and Idaho. In 1899 he was made a member of the national executive board of the Western Federation of Miners and a year later was selected secretary-treasurer. In 1905, by which time he had become a crusader for industrial unionism and Socialism (he joined the Socialist Party of America in 1901), he took part in the founding of the I. W. W. Arrested a few months later on a charge of having helped plot the murder of Frank Steunenberg, former governor of Idaho, he was acquitted after a period of fifteen months' imprisonment during which he ran as Socialist candidate for governor of Colorado.

Until 1913, although he continued to work for the I. W. W., Haywood's energies were expended primarily on behalf of the Socialist Party. He became a contributing editor of the *International Socialist Review,* lectured widely throughout the United States, campaigned vigorously for Debs during the 1908 presidential race, served as a delegate to the International Socialist Congress at Copenhagen in 1910, and in 1911 was elected to the Socialist Party's national executive committee. But in 1913, because of his emphasis on direct action and sabotage, he was

---

*Georges Sorel (1847–1922), a French engineer turned social philosopher, was the chief theoretician of syndicalism—the idea of workers' control, of a radical industrial democracy. A critic of both traditional liberalism and socialism, Sorel desired to supplant the bourgeois state with a corporate one, with a structure based on syndicates of workers identified by occupation and, as the only productive class in society, enjoying the rewards of power.

recalled from the party's national executive committee.* It was only after this break with the Socialists that he emerged as the symbolic and real leader of the apolitical, syndicalist, and revolutionary I. W. W. The high point of his efficiency as a union administrator and as a spell-binding advocate of revolution corresponded with that organization's heyday. At the time of his 1918 conviction the "tall Cyclops" was clearly the most outstanding and glamorous personality among the Wobblies.

One important consequence of Haywood's experience as a Socialist Party politician was that it left him profoundly disillusioned with the ability of American Marxists to make a revolution. It was his conviction that the only effective way of making the working class revolutionary was by leading its members in persistent struggle against the capitalists in all segments of industrial life. Hence, while he did not repudiate political action altogether (wishing to use industrial unionism as a source of constant pressure on state and local governments in alliance with capitalism), he felt that participation in electoral contests and in the affairs of government would corrupt the workers unless they were guided by a militant and revolutionary industrial unionist movement. The coming proletarian society which Haywood envisioned would be based not on a political party but on the trade union movement. Through their unions the workers would acquire control of industry and replace capitalist politicians and parliaments with direct agencies of their industrial power.

Similar to most of the I. W. W.'s members, "Big Bill" was neither an original thinker nor a theoretician. While one might quarrel with Max Eastman's judgment that Haywood's "mind was feminine and childlike," it is certainly true that he "sensed things better than he understood them, and was more at home in figurative than analytic language." Without formal education and uncomfortable with abstractions, he is best described as an activist and a pragmatist (qualities which prompted the *Nation* to characterize him "as American as Bret Harte or Mark Twain")

*Haywood was expelled under Article 2, Section 6, of the party constitution, which unequivocally demanded the expulsion of members who instead of political action favored or "advocated sabotage or other methods of violence as a weapon of the working class."

who must be remembered more for what he revealed of the frustrations of American radicals in the industrial age than for what he contributed to the dialogue of the early twentieth century on the nature of society.[2]

Haywood was aware that whoever held power ruled society, and he therefore stressed the necessity of transferring power from the capitalists to the workers. Yet he never publicly called upon the proletariat to take up arms. It was not that he was a pacifist; on the contrary, he believed that there were times when the workers could not avoid responding in kind to the capitalists' use of force. But he had come to realize that violence should be avoided whenever possible, for it was both unproductive (it could lead to violent reprisals) and unnecessary (all that the proletariat need do to achieve their goals was to refuse to work). Indeed, by 1913 Haywood was maintaining that "labor wars of the old type are passing." "I for one have turned my back on violence. It wins nothing. When we strike now, we strike with our hands in our pockets. We have a new kind of violence—the havoc we raise with money by laying down our tools. Our strength lies in the overwhelming power of our numbers."[3]

If reasons of expediency prompted Haywood to reject "labor wars," he condemned wars between states on the grounds that they were capitalist conflicts in which the workers had no stake. What was the "state" to the workers but the tool of their capitalist oppressors? Why risk life and limb in the defense of the class enemy? It was to one another, not to nations, that the workers owed their loyalty. As Haywood related at a dinner party in New York City, recalled years later by Hutchins Hapgood, "in the solidarity of the workers there is no France, Germany, Russia, or the United States," but "only international humanity which wipes away prejudice and ignorance and brings men together in essential unity."

Haywood's exhortations on behalf of workers' solidarity were often accompanied by denunciations of patriotism—denunciations, which even before the outbreak of the First World War, provoked considerable antagonism. In February 1914, for example, as a consequence of Haywood's antipatriotic assertions before a meeting of the International Socialist League ("We don't care for the flag, and we are against patriotism. We have learned that the American flag is not our flag. There is only one flag in the world for us, and that is the red flag."), he was barred by the New York City Board of Education from participating in a previously scheduled discussion on labor in Brooklyn's Manual Training School. "William D. Haywood," announced board member Francis P. Cunnion, "will not be permitted to speak . . . in any public school in this city. A man, who talks as he does, of the American flag, can not be allowed to address public school children, one of whose duties is daily to salute the flag. To permit him to do so would be a comedy of errors."[4]

Haywood's solution to the problem of how wars between states might be averted was a logical offshoot of his faith in workers' solidarity: the general strike. He was the only one of the twenty-four American delegates at the International Socialist Congress at Copenhagen in 1910 to support the following resolution proposed by the French leader Jean Jaurès: "Among all the means of preventing and stopping war and of compelling governments to resort to arbitration, the congress considers as particularly efficacious the general strike simultaneously and internationally organized in all the countries concerned." And in 1914 Haywood still regarded the general strike as "the only guarantee of peace." In April of that year he told an audience in New York's Carnegie Hall that the moment President Wilson and the Congress declared war against Mexico, the "workers will simply fold their arms, and when they fold their arms there will be no war." Five months later, following the outbreak of war in Europe, he complained that "If the diplomats, statesmen and parliamentarians of the Socialist movement could have realized with Jaurès the power of the general strike . . . the terrible carnage would have been averted."[5]

Haywood greeted the war in Europe with bitter criticism of that great majority of European socialists who supported the belligerency of their respective governments. When he was questioned in Washington, D. C., before the Industrial Relations Committee, formed to examine the industrial unrest of the period, he commented that he would prefer his interrogator to "eliminate the reference to Socialism" in referring to the I. W. W., "because from the examples we have, for instance, in Germany, Socialism . . . has been very much discredited in the minds of workers of other countries. They have gone in for war, and those of us who believe we are Socialists are opposed to war." Yet, such castigations of European Socialism notwithstanding, Haywood later admitted in his autobiography that once the conflict was under way, "he never felt any doubt about the United States becoming involved." Despite all his talk of a general strike, he believed, together with most other Wobbly leaders, that there was not much that could be done to prevent American participation. The I. W. W. might adopt antiwar resolutions—as it did at its 1914 and 1916 conventions—but it never seriously believed that it could spare American workers the horrors of the battlefield. As the I. W. W. newspaper, *Solidarity,* predicted in the fall of 1914, sooner or later the "economic laws of the system" were "bound to plunge America into war." The consquence of this fatalistic attitude was that, except for stating its opposition to war, the I. W. W. did nothing concrete to organize workers in opposition to American intervention. On the contrary, it took the position that the workers should concentrate their attention on preparing for the class struggle which was certain to erupt following the war's end. Hence, the I. W. W. substituted words for positive action. Wobbly soapboxers attacked the European debacle as an object lesson in capitalist folly, while a popular I. W. W. sticker issued in 1916 enjoined workers

Don't Be a Soldier. Be a Man.
Join the I. W. W. and fight on the job for yourself and your class.

"We have not ceased to carry on the usual campaign against militarism," Haywood wrote to a fellow Wobbly in Spokane, Washington, "[but] our members should also realize that they are in a bitter war, the class war. . . ."[6]

At the beginning of 1917, Haywood informed Leo Lauke, editor of Duluth, Minnesota's Finnish I. W. W. daily, *Industrialisti,* that America's steady approach toward involvement in the European conflagration "looks like a move to save the life of Germany. If involved in a world wide war, Germany could make peace, which she feels she cannot do now without stultifying herself and acknowledging her defeat." The comment was an

unusual one, for, from late 1914 to the summer of 1917, the
I. W. W.'s secretary-treasurer wrote very little either on the war
or with regard to militarism. Although he continued to serve as
a contributing editor of the *International Socialist Review* during the period in question, he published in that journal only one
vaguely war-related item—a brief and far from profound plea on
behalf of "Everlasting Peace":

To insure "peace on earth, good will to men," reverse the present order
of things.
Let no man pray for another man.
Let no man make laws for another man.
Let no man fight for another man.
Let no man keep money for another man.
Let no man block the opportunities of another man.
Let no man appropriate that which is produced by another man.
Let every man put his hands to the bounteous treasures of the earth, and
from his brains will spring forth marvelous machinery that will feed and
clothe and house and educate the children of the world in "peace and
good will."

Haywood was spending most of his time taking advantage of
the remarkable I. W. W. resurgence encouraged by the war in
Europe. War orders had led to increased production, higher
profits, and a growing scarcity of labor—circumstances which
enabled the I. W. W. both to organize successfully and to obtain
material improvements for its members, since few employers
were willing "to sacrifice wartime profits to anti-union principles."[7]

Shortly after the United States entered the war, Haywood
expressed his concern to newspaperman John Beffel that the
conflict would "give the flag-wavers and the A. F. of L. a chance
to throw rocks at the I. W. W. That'll be sport for Gompers."
But he noted that what most distressed him was the way the
country had been "dragged in" to the European folly. "There'll
have to be conscription. Not enough men will volunteer to
break up a *Sängerfest*. After that, bloody horrors enough to
satisfy all the stay-at-home patriots. And it will be the blood of
the workers."

Yet, if Haywood was upset by the prospects which American

intervention held for the I. W. W. and the nation's workers, he opposed transforming the I. W. W. into an antiwar organization, persisting in the conviction that it must remain first and always a labor union. Accordingly, when fiery Frank Little argued that the organization should take a strong stand against enlistment, Haywood counseled him: "Keep a cool head; do not talk. A good many feel as you do but the world war is of small importance compared to the great class war. I am at a loss as to definite steps to be taken against the war."[8]

In urging "a cool head," Haywood was in agreement with the dominant group in the I. W. W.'s General Executive Board, which opposed anything more than a general condemnation of American involvement. For one thing, the majority reasoned, there was too much work to be done organizing miners, harvest hands, and other laborers to undertake a spirited campaign against the war. For another, they realized that if the I. W. W. challenged the United States war effort—even to the limited extent of endorsing a policy of refusing to register and refusing to fight—they would bring upon the organization the wrath of the American public. Hence, while agreeing unanimously that the war was tragic and wholly wrong, the union's leadership purposefully refrained from adopting any policies intended to impede the nation's war effort. When, in the summer of 1917, the head of the Construction Workers Industrial Union No. 573 requested a statement of the I. W. W.'s stand on registering for the draft, Haywood informed him: "No official stand has been taken by the Organization on the question of registration, believing that the individual member was the best judge of how to act upon this question."[9]

Apparently, the individual consciences of most draft-age Wobblies dictated service to country, for approximately ninety-five percent of them registered with their draft boards, and the great majority of those who registered served when called. While there were some members who agitated against the draft, refused to register, or fled the country, it would appear that in only two areas did Wobblies take part in significant antiwar demonstrations: in Rockford, Illinois, where roughly one hundred nonregistrants protested the war in front of the city hall, and on the Mesabi Iron Range in Minnesota, where a sizable number of Finnish emigrés employed as miners refused conscription.[10]

As the wartime hysteria against dissenters mounted, Haywood went beyond simply counseling I. W. W. members to maintain a hands-off policy toward America's role in the conflict and sought to restrain or curtail the organization's more incendiary antimilitarist propaganda. He suspended the "Sab Cat" cartoon which had freely appeared in *Solidarity* to symbolize the tactic of "slowing down" as a means of "striking on the job"; he called a stop to the printing of "The Deadly Parallel," a bulletin contrasting the antiwar sentiments of the I. W. W. with the pro-war stand of the A. F. L.; he even deleted some of the more "offensive" songs from the wartime editions of the union's "Little Red Songbook," such as John F. Kendrick's "Christians at War," a satirical imitation of "Onward Christian Soldiers:"

> Onward, Christian soldiers! Duty's way is plain;
> Slay your Christian neighbors, or by them be slain.
> Pulpiteers are spouting effervescent swill,
> God above is calling you to rob and rape and kill,
> All your acts are sanctified by the Lamb on high;
> If you love the Holy Ghost, go murder, pray and die.
>
> Onward, Christian soldiers, rip and tear and smite!
> Let the gentle Jesus bless your dynamite.
> Splinter skulls with shrapnel, fertilize the sod;
> Folks who do not speak your tongue deserve the curse of God.
> Smash the doors of every home, pretty maidens seize;
> Use your might and sacred right to treat them as you please.
>
> Onward, Christian soldiers! Eat and drink your fill;
> Rob with bloody fingers, Christ O. K.'s the bill.
> Steal the farmer's savings, take their grain and meat;
> Even though the children starve, the Saviour's bums must eat.
> Burn the peasants' cottages, orphans leave bereft;
> In Jehovah's holy name, wreak ruin right and left.
>
> Onward, Christian soldiers! Drench the land with gore;
> Mercy is a weakness all the gods abhor.
> Bayonet the babies, jab the mothers, too;
> Hoist the cross of Calvary to hallow all you do.
> File your bullets' noses flat, poison every well;
> God decrees your enemies must all go plumb to hell.
>
> Onward, Christian soldiers! Blighting all you meet,
> Trampling human freedom under pious feet.

Praise the Lord whose dollar-sign dupes his favored race!
Make the foreign trash respect your bullion brand of grace.
Trust in mock salvation, serve as pirates' tools;
History will say of you: "That pack of G— d— fools."[11]

Unfortunately for the I. W. W., Haywood's efforts to soften the organization's image were in vain. During the spring and summer of 1917, I. W. W. strikes threatened the wheat harvest of the Midwest, the copper mines of Montana and Arizona, and the lumber industry from Sand Point, Idaho, to the Douglas fir forests of Puget Sound. Although they thus affected industries vital to the American war effort, there is no evidence that these strikes were intended as anything more than a means of improving working conditions. Yet, accusations were made which received credence in the Justice and War Departments that they were financed by German gold.[12] United States Senator Henry Ashurst, Democrat of Arizona, mirrored the sentiments of many Americans when he said on the Senate floor: "I have frequently been asked what 'IWW' means. It means simply, solely, and only 'Imperial Wilhelm's Warriors.' "[13] "If German agents or not," maintained the editor of an Idaho newspaper, "they might as well be on the Kaiser's payroll as anybody now interfering with U. S. industry is lending comfort to Germany."[14]

In reality, the I. W. W. was not pro-German. Nor was it an alien-dominated organization which "intended to poison the canned goods used by the army" and was "responsible for the spread of hoof and mouth disease" among cattle.[15] But, however outlandish, such charges seemed quite plausible to thousands of Americans who were convinced that the I. W. W. was bent on hindering the war effort at all costs. It is not surprising that people who could accept the type of "justice" which resulted in more than 1000 striking miners being forcibly deported from Bisbee, Arizona, to the Hermanas Desert and allowed the six Montana "vigilantes" who murdered Wobbly leader Frank Little on 1 August 1917 to remain unapprehended, would reject Haywood's denial that German influence had anything to do with the union's activities:

It is true that we think there is only one fight in the world, and that is between capital and labor. It is true that we are not interested in nationalities.

We will fight for German workers or French workers or Norwegian workers just as hard as we will for American workers. But do you think we want to see the Prussian military system prevail? How would we stand to gain anything from that?

. . . It is because the employing interests fear its growth that they are bringing out the charge of German influence. It's a new weapon and a handy one, but nevertheless merely another of the many false and baseless charges that have been brought against the organization.[16]

The public unease engendered by the I. W. W.'s alleged pro-Germanism, its revolutionary ideology, and its success in "organizing on the job" in the industries of the West resulted in its becoming a major target of the nation-wide campaign to suppress radical labor movements which followed America's entry into the war. On the morning of 5 September 1917, Justice Department agents and local police officers raided the organization's central headquarters in Chicago and Wobbly halls in over a dozen other cities throughout the nation. Armed with perhaps the broadest search warrants ever issued by the American judiciary, the invaders confiscated many tons of materials—including not only letters, newspapers, pamphlets, and other documents, but even desks and typewriters. Three weeks later, Haywood, all other members of the union's General Executive Board, and over one hundred less prominent Wobblies were indicted in the Chicago federal court for conspiracies to obstruct the Selective Service Act and to violate the Espionage Act. The indictment—a document of thirty-two pages—comprised five counts:

1. Conspiracy "by force to prevent hinder and delay the execution of certain laws of the United States"—namely all the resolutions and acts of congress passed between April 6 and June 16, 1917, with reference to the war with Germany, the appropriations therefore, etc. The second part of the same count charges that the defendants, as members of the I. W. W., . . . had engaged in the alleged conspiracy and had employed felonious and forcible means, . . . knowing and intending that such acts and methods should interfere with the effective prosecution of the war; that they had required members to refuse to register or submit to the draft. . . .
2. Conspiracy to injure, oppress and threaten great numbers of citizens who had been engaged in furnishing ships, fuel, munitions, etc., to the United States for its operations against Germany.
3. Conspiracy to induce or compel thousands to refuse to register or submit to the draft, and to induce or command other thousands to desert the service of the government in time of war.

4. Conspiracy to print or circulate disloyal, seditious and unpatriotic literature and periodicals, and to cause insubordination and disloyalty by means of publications or speeches.
5. Conspiracy to violate the postal laws by putting in the mails papers and circulars which advocated fraud against employers by means of sabotage, inefficient service, retardation of production, the turning out of unmarketable commodities, etc. [This count was dismissed by Judge K. M. Landis on the last day of the 1918 trial, just before the case was submitted to the jury.] [17]

Shortly after Haywood was arrested and imprisoned together with 165 other Wobblies in Chicago's antiquated Cook County jail, he reacted to charges against the I. W. W. in an interview with Carl Sandburg. "[We have] done nothing on the war one way or another," he insisted. "It is true we have called strikes, but they were not aimed at stopping the war." He was equally emphatic in denying that the I. W. W. had accepted German money—an allegation which, though not contained in the indictment, he knew to be particularly damaging to the union's public image: "Not a dirty German dollar has ever come into our hands that we know of. . . . Every dollar we've got now and every dollar the organization will get comes from workingmen." In these disclaimers the I. W. W.'s secretary-treasurer was supported, albeit ineffectually, by a fairly large number of American radicals who, like the editors of the newspaper *Michigan Socialist,* believed that the arrest and jailing of Wobbly Leaders was "but a blind to conceal the government's real aim to crush organizations who insist upon telling the truth about the war and peace." "Whether one relishes it or not," maintained the energetic young Socialist Louis Fraina, "the fact is that the I. W. W. has not acted against the war . . . and is chiefly if not exclusively at the moment interested in questions of wages and the regulation of industrial conditions." [18]

Outside radical circles, however, there were not many persons during the seven months separating the I. W. W. raids and the trial who challenged openly the accuracy of the government's charges; and there were fewer still who agreed with Helen Keller that the social system that produced the I. W. W. was far more deserving of indictment than "those who are struggling mightily against the greatest evils of the age." As Ralph Chaplin later commented in recalling press coverage of the raids, "After reading

the sensational newspaper accounts of our villainy, I sometimes
doubted my own innocence." Robert W. Bruère's opinion of the
"alleged I. W. W. conspiracy" in Arizona was conspicuous for
the infrequency with which such assertions appeared in the pages
of the establishment press: "If such a conspiracy existed . . . I
am certain that it was not a determining factor in the strikes
that tied up the copper mines. . . . Crimes have been committed
in Arizona, but they are not chargeable to the I. W. W."

On 1 April 1918, 113 of the 166 Wobblies indicted during
the previous September were placed on trial in Chicago before
Judge Kenesaw Mountain Landis, soon to become famous in
the aftermath of the 1919 Black Sox scandal as baseball's first
commissioner. Described by the hostile pen of John Reed, who
covered the affair for the *Liberator,* as possessing "the face of
Andrew Jackson three years dead," Landis had earlier presided
over the trial of a group of Wobblies and Socialists from Rockford, Illinois, accused of evading the Registration Act. Although
he had a son in the army and was strongly supportive of the
American war effort, Landis conducted the Chicago proceedings
in a commendably impartial manner, providing the defendants
every right or privilege to which they were legally entitled. The
harsh sentences which he imposed on the defendants on 31
August 1918 contrasted sharply with the judicial objectivity he
displayed during the five tiring months of what was at that time
the longest criminal trial in the country's history. Even Haywood
had no fault to find with Landis's conduct of the trial. "He was
fair to us, absolutely square throughout the whole trial," the
I. W. W. leader told a reporter thirteen days prior to sentencing.
"His instructions were fair, I thought, and certainly he treated
us excellently while the trial was in progress."[19]

As Melvyn Dubofsky points out in his lengthy history of
the I. W. W., despite "the hysterical propaganda and the massive
federal raids that preceded it," the Chicago trial was a rather
dull affair in which "nothing original or startling came to light."
Perhaps the biggest surprise in the proceedings was that the
chief counsel for the defense, Seattle attorney George F. Vanderveer, chose not to offer a closing argument to the jury. While
the reasons for this decision have never been adequately explained
Dubofsky's conjecture may be near the truth:

. . . it does not seem improbable that Vanderveer had nothing to say in a summation that he had not already said or established more effectively during his examination and cross-examination of witnesses. Moreover, it appears likely that Vanderveer honestly believed the prosecution had failed to adduce evidence that would lead a jury to convict an individual defendant; since the organization, in theory, was not on trial, the defense had no reason to present a final rebuttal. In other words, Vanderveer probably assumed that whatever decision the jury reached, it could hardly be based upon the evidence offered by the government.

Whatever the bases of his decision, Vanderveer's subsequent complaint that the defendants were tried not for their own sanctions —not even for their own beliefs—but rather for what the government claimed to be the beliefs of the organization to which they belonged, is well grounded. Yet, in fairness, it should be added that the I. W. W. was itself not entirely blameless on this score. On the eve of the trial Vanderveer was told that, since the union's General Defense Committee had decided to use the courtroom as a sounding board for I. W. W. arguments, he was to defend the accused not as individuals but as disciples of a great cause. Accordingly, as the *Christian Science Monitor* accurately noted, Vanderveer both encouraged the defendants to engage in "propaganda speechmaking" and used tactics designed "to keep the jury interested." Instead of concentrating on proving the innocence of individual defendants, he directed much effort toward portraying them as disciples of a great cause. For example, he got around Landis's ruling that evidence relating to exploitative working conditions was inadmissible by having defendants testify about personal experiences in which "capitalist exploitation" was an overriding theme.[20]

The highlight of the trial was the testimony of its central figure, "Big Bill" Haywood, to whom the prosecution referred alternately as the "swivel chair king" of an effort to upset the nation's military program and the "Commander in Chief of the biggest anti-war conspiracy in all history."[21] During his four days on the stand the I. W. W.'s controversial secretary-treasurer, while admitting both that he was "very much opposed to war" and that he believed "the workers have no country," stated among other things that he could "not recall a single word or a line" that he had written, or "a thought" that he had possessed, to hamper

the American war effort. Haywood maintained that "the aim
and purpose" of the literature which he and other Wobblies had
distributed since the United States joined the struggle across
the Atlantic was not to destroy the idea of patriotism, but rather
"to disseminate the ideal of industrialism, . . . to build, to con-
struct; the Industrial Workers of the World is not a destructive
organization but a constructive one." When asked whether he
and the other defendants had conspired to interfere with the
profits of persons engaged in the manufacture of munitions, he
replied:

We are conspiring to prevent the making of profits on labor power in any
industry. We are conspiring against the dividend makers. We are conspiring
against rent and interest. We want to establish a new society, where people
can live without profit, without dividends, without rent and without interest if it is possible; and it is possible, if people will live normally, live
like human beings should live. I would say that if that is a conspiracy,
we are conspiring.

Haywood was especially emphatic in countering prosecutor
Frank L. Nebeker's assertion that I. W. W. members had been
expelled for enlisting in military service.[22] The Wobbly leader
pointed out that there was no record of such expulsions, that
there was no clause in the union's constitution providing for any
and that a number of members were currently fighting in France.
Moreover, cautioning the prosecution that neither the antiwar
resolutions adopted by local I. W. W. branches nor the anticonscription declarations of the late Frank Little should be taken
as representing the views of the general organization, he stated:
"It was not for me, a man who could not be drafted, to advise
any one else to go, or not to go."

Considering that Haywood was never at his best in situations
which demanded facile thought and expression, his courtroom
performance was creditable. If, as his codefendant Richard
Brazier later lamented, he "did not have the old fire . . . and
occasionally had to be asked to speak a little louder," he was
nonetheless a good witness, responding fully and without hesi-
tation to most of the questions asked him. What he lacked in
"fire," he made up for in sincerity.[23]

On 17 August 1918, after deliberating for less than an hour,

the jury returned a verdict of guilty for one hundred defendants*
charged on four separate counts with having committed over ten
thousand crimes. Reflecting the high degree of public interest in
the case, the jury's decision was headlined on the first page of
the following day's *Chicago Sunday Tribune:* "Convict 100
I. W. W. Chiefs: Jurors Find Disloyalists Hampered War."

Two weeks later, Judge Landis sentenced the defendants to
varying terms of imprisonment and imposed on them fines total-
ing in excess of $2,000,000. Haywood was fined $10,000 and,
together with fourteen others, was sentenced to prison for the
legal maximum of twenty years. Landis supported the harsh
treatment accorded the convicted "conspirators" with the following statement:

Now, I do not mean to say that this organization deliberately started
out to organize in the United States to help Germany. Whether some members of this organization had that in mind or not I am without opinion,
which is unnecessary, if I had one, to express on this occasion. But that
the activities of the organization were necessarily and reasonably calculated to obstruct the activities of the United States, not only in the enforcement of the Compulsory Service Law requiring registration on June 5,
but to obstruct the activities of the United States in providing itself with
war equipment, there can be no kind of doubt.

And when men engaged in an enterprise of that character are placed on
trial and the proofs brought out there is only one thing for a jury to do,
and that is to find them guilty. The jury could not have done anything else
on this evidence but find a verdict of guilty. . . .

When the country is at peace it is a legal right of free speech to oppose
going to war and to oppose even preparation for war. But when once war
is declared this right ceases. After war is declared and before the law was
passed to raise the army it was the legal right of free speech to oppose the
adoption of a compulsory military service law. But once that law was
passed free speech did not authorize a man to oppose or resist that law.
The man that opposes it or resists it violates it, and men who conspire to
aid another man to oppose or resist it violate the statute penalizing conspiracy. . . .

Although Haywood had no quarrel with Landis's conduct
while the trial was in progress, he attacked the severe sentences

---

*During the course of the trial the government dismissed its case against thirteen
of the original defendants. One of those discharged, A. C. Christ, had appeared before
the court on April 1 in military uniform.

which the judge imposed as a "sadistic carnival" motivated not only by "patriotism," but also by "revenge" for having caused the latter "to miss so many ball games." Moreover, he steadfastly refused to admit that he or the other defendants were in any sense guilty of the crimes for which they had been convicted. For example, in October 1920, when the United States Circuit Court of Appeals confirmed the 1918 verdict, he told a New York audience: "We were convicted because we were against war. . . . But we did not conspire to prevent war, or to keep this country from entering the war."[24]

Considering that Haywood had on occasion referred to the American soldier as "a boil on the body politic," it is perhaps ironic that the most persuasive support for his protestations of innocence came from one Alexander S. Lanier who, as a captain in the army's military intelligence division, had observed the courtroom proceedings in Chicago and had then made a careful summary of the evidence. A lawyer in civilian life and a self-professed member of society's "upper crust," Lanier wrote an open letter to President Wilson, in which he maintained that the government's evidence was insufficient to establish a conspiracy. "I am of the opinion that these men were convicted contrary to the law and the evidence, solely because they were leaders in a revolutionary organization against which public sentiment was incensed and the verdict rendered was in obedience to public hysteria and popular demand. . . ."[25]

As most Americans saw it, however, Haywood and the other "Bolsheviki of America" tried in Chicago were proven disloyalists who fully deserved the stiff penalties they had received. Popular opinion was very much in tune with the sentiment expressed by the editors of *World's Work:* "We should show as little mercy to internal agitators caught committing these acts as the Huns who destroy women and children and who seek to annihilate democratic civilization."[26] The persistence of such a view helped to insure that the I. W. W. would never again play the prominent role in the nation's labor movement that it had enjoyed prior to 1918.

Following his sentencing by Judge Landis, Haywood was released on $30,000 bail, pending a decision on the application for a new trial. In March 1921, perhaps fearful of the effects of a prison term on his declining health (he was plagued by a history of ulcers, diabetes, and possibly cirrhosis of the liver), Haywood jumped bail and fled to the Soviet Union. Although received at first warmly by the Bolshevik government, which granted him a pension, he was given little to do of any importance and lived out the remainder of his days in relative obscurity—"cast on the refuse pile," as fellow-exile Emma Goldman had predicted shortly after the ailing Wobbly arrived in Russia.[27] Following his death in May 1928, his ashes were divided between the Kremlin Wall (alongside those of John Reed) and Chicago's Waldheim Cemetery.

William D. Haywood was as genuinely opposed to the First World War as were Eugene Debs and Emma Goldman. He regarded that conflict as unfortunate, tragic, and utterly wrong. But he attempted to subordinate his personal feelings about what should be done to resist it to the best interests of the radical labor union he represented. If, in the end, his efforts to save the I. W. W. proved unsuccessful, that is less an indictment of the man than a reflection of the public hysteria with which he and other antiwar radicals were forced to contend.

AN AFTERWORD

The story related in the preceding pages, if in some respects inspiring, is also a discomforting one. The antiwar stand taken by the six American radicals in question represents at one and the same time all that was finest and all that was weakest and most ineffective in the peace movement of yesterday. However sympathetic one may be to their stalwart and idealistic opposition to authority in a time of social crisis, the fact remains that their struggle—and that of thousands of others whose feelings and ideas they expressed—was futile; it must be judged a failure. Despite all they said and did, they could not stem the tide of events. America entered the bloody struggle across the Atlantic, conscription was introduced, and the government abridged the civil liberties and rights of citizens with a more dogged determination than at any time in the nation's history except the Civil War.

The irony of the harsh repression of the voices opposed to the First World War is that within twenty years of the conflict's end a majority of Americans regarded the intervention an error. When George Gallup took a nationwide poll in 1937 on the question of whether the United States had been mistaken in entering the World War, seventy percent of those polled responded in the affirmative. Americans of the 1930s were aware of the war's human and material price—a price that those of their countrymen who supported intervention in 1917 could have foreseen only in the most horrifying of nightmares. During the less than two years that the nation was engaged in this "war to end wars," some 53,000 American soldiers died in combat, another 63,000 died of disease, and over 200,000 were wounded. Moreover, in support of all this death and human suffering the United States spent thirty-five billion dollars—ten times more than during the Civil War and as much every two days as the entire cost of the Revolutionary War.

NOTES

INTRODUCTION

1.　Merle Curti et al., *An American History* (New York: Harper, 1950), vol. 2, p. 159.

2.　Merle Curti, *The Roots of American Loyalty* (New York: Columbia University Press, 1946), p. 152.

3.　*Congressional Globe,* 29th Congress, 2d Session, Appendix (11 February 1847).

4.　As quoted in James R. Shirley, "War Protest in Wartime," *New Republic,* 6 May 1967, p. 15.

5.　*Speeches, Correspondence and Political Papers of Carl Schurz.* Edited by Frederic Bancroft (New York: G. P. Putnam's Sons, 1913), vol. 6, pp. 77-79.

6.　Senator John Sharp Williams of Mississippi as quoted in H. C. Peterson and Gilbert C. Fite, *Opponents of War, 1917-1918* (Madison: University of Wisconsin Press, 1957), p. 6.

7.　Ibid., pp. 79 and 116.

8.　"War and Freedom," *Common Sense,* May 1943, p. 157.

9.　*New York Times* of 3 August and 15 September 1950.

1: EUGENE V. DEBS, MISSIONARY OF AMERICAN SOCIALISM

1.　Ruth Le Prade, ed., *Debs and the Poets* (Pasadena: Upton Sinclair, 1920), p. 6; Herbert M. Morais and William Cahn, *Gene Debs* (New York: International Publishers, 1948), p. 10; Frank Harris, *Latest Contemporary Portraits* (New York: Macaulay, 1927), pp. 103-04; "Eugene Victor Debs," *Nation,* 3 November 1926, p. 443; Max Lerner, *The Mind and Faith of Justice Holmes* (Boston: Little, Brown, 1943), p. 442; *New York Times,* 9 July 1894; *Outlook,* 11 May 1921, p. 49.

2.　*Speeches of Eugene V. Debs* (New York: International Publishers, 1928), p. 22. Trachtenberg was a native of Russia who had taken part in the Revolution of 1905. He emigrated to the United States in 1906 and played an important role in the Intercollegiate Socialist Society, first at Trinity College and then at Yale University. In 1915 he went to New York to head the Research Department of the Rand School of Social Science and to edit the *American Labor Year Book.* He later became a Communist and founded International Publishers.

3.　Bertha K. Ehrmann, "Reminiscences of Max Ehrmann," *Indiana Magazine of History,* September 1950, p. 249.

4.   Daniel Bell, "Marxian Socialism in the United States," in Donald D. Egbert and Stow Persons, eds., *Socialism and American Life* (Princeton: Princeton University Press, 1952), vol. 1, p. 295.

5.   *Speeches of E. V. Debs, Social Democratic Candidate for President, and Professor George D. Herron, Central Music Hall, Chicago, September 29* (Chicago: n.p., 1900), p. 2; David Karsner, *Debs* (New York: Boni and Liveright, 1919), pp. 203–04.

6.   "Soldiers, Slaves and Hell," *Iron City Socialist* (Pittsburgh), 14 March 1914; *American Socialist,* 5 September 1914.

7.   *New York Call,* 9 August 1914; "Anti-War Manifestoes," *New Review,* September 1914, pp. 523–24; Alexander Trachtenberg, ed., *The American Socialists and the War* (New York: Rand School of Social Science, 1917), pp. 10–17.

8.   "Socialists and the War," *National Rip-Saw,* September 1914; "International Patriotism," ibid., November 1914; *American Socialist,* 31 October 1914.

9.   *American Socialist,* 26 September and 28 November 1914, 9 January 1915.

10.   Oscar Ameringer, *If You Don't Weaken* (New York: Henry Holt, 1940), p. 268; *American Socialist,* 31 October 1914; "Churchmen and the War," *National Rip-Saw,* December 1914.

11.   " 'Preparedness' I Favor," *Appeal to Reason,* 11 December 1915; "American Militarism," *National Rip-Saw,* January 1915; "Peace 'With Honor,' " *American Socialist,* 11 March 1916. See also David A. Shannon, *The Socialist Party of America* (New York: Macmillan, 1955), p. 89.

12.   "Politicians and Preachers," *American Socialist,* 24 June 1916; Debs to Upton Sinclair, 12 June 1916, *Upton Sinclair MSS,* Lilly Library, Indiana University.

13.   Trachtenberg, p. 14.

14.   *American Socialist,* 22 April 1916.

15.   Debs to Daniel Hoan, 17 August 1916. *Debs Collection,* Tamiment Library, New York City (hereafter cited as *DC*).

16.   H. Scott Bennett, "Will Eugene V. Debs Sit in Congress?," *International Socialist Review,* September 1916, p. 145.

17.   "Socialist Anti-War Meetings," *American Socialist,* 17 March 1917.

18.   "Peace on Earth," ibid., 9 January 1915; "Preparedness and Poverty," ibid., 18 December 1915; *Socialist Hand Book, Campaign 1916* (Chicago: Socialist Party, 1916), p. 7; *New York Times,* 8 March 1917.

19.   "Schwab's Palace and Preparedness," *American Socialist,* 4 March 1916; "The Gunmen and the Miners," *International Socialist Review,* September 1914, p. 162; "When I Shall Fight," *Appeal to Reason,* 11 September 1915; " 'Preparedness' and Poverty," *American Socialist,* 18 December 1915.

20.   For the full text of the St. Louis Proclamation see *American Labor Year Book, 1917-18.* Edited by Alexander Trachtenberg (New York: Rand School of Social Science, 1918), pp. 50–53.

21.   *New York Call,* 8 July 1917. In a letter to Secretary of State Robert Lansing, dated 11 May 1917, Wilson referred to the "almost treasonable utterances" of the Socialists of St. Louis. Ray stannard Baker, *Woodrow Wilson,* vol. 7: *War Leader* (Garden City: Doubleday, Doran & Co., 1939), p. 65.

22.   "The Majority Report," *American Socialist,* 26 May 1917.

23.   *New York Times,* 28 June 1917; Ray Ginger, *The Bending Cross* (New Brunswick: Rutgers University Press, 1949), p. 347.

24.   *New York Times,* 14 August 1917; Frank L. Grubbs, Jr., "Council and Alliance Labor Propaganda: 1917-1919," *Labor History,* Spring 1966, pp. 156-57, 165. The American Alliance for Labor and Democracy was founded in New York City in June 1917, and the following September it expanded into a national body. Its members believed that "war waged for evil ends must be met by war waged for altruistic ends," and maintained that "where expressions are used which are obstructive to the government in its conduct of the war. . . , the offenders should be repressed by the constituted authorities in accordance with established law." (James Oneal, "The Socialists in the War," *American Mercury,* April 1927, p. 422.)

25.   Christopher Lasch, *The American Liberals and the Russian Revolution* (New York: Columbia University Press, 1962), p. 99; Morris Hillquit, *Loose Leaves from a Busy Life* (New York: Macmillan, 1934), p. 235.

26.   "A Personal Statement," unidentified newspaper clipping dated May 1918, in *Eugene Debs Scrapbook,* 10 (1915-20), *DC.*

27.   Hillquit, p. 235.

28.   Harry N. Schreiber, *The Wilson Administration and Civil Liberties* (Ithaca: Cornell University Press, 1960), p. 23; Theodore Roosevelt, *Roosevelt in the Kansas City Star* (Boston and New York: Houghton Mifflin, 1921), pp. 2 and 56; *New York Times,* 9 June 1917; Mark Sullivan, *Our Times: The United States, 1900-1925,* vol. 5: *Over Here, 1914-1918* (New York: Charles Scribner's Sons, 1933), p. 468; O. A. Hilton, "Public Opinion and Civil Liberties in Wartime 1917-1919," *Southwestern Social Science Quarterly,* December 1947, p. 207.

29.   McAlister Coleman, *Eugene V. Debs* (New York: Greenberg, 1930), p. 284.

30.   Clyde R. Miller, "The Man I Sent to Jail," *Say* (Chicago: Alumni Quarterly of Roosevelt University), Winter 1954,p. 71; Bernard J. Brommel, "The Pacifist Speechmaking of Eugene V. Debs," *Quarterly Journal of Speech,* April 1966, p. 148.

31.   Debs's Canton, Ohio, speech is printed in full in *The Debs White Book* (Girard, Kansas: Appeal to Reason, n.d.), pp. 3-36.

32.   Shannon, p. 114.

33.   *Cleveland Plain Dealer,* 17 June 1918; *Cleveland Press,* 19 June 1918.

34.   *Indianapolis News,* 18 and 24 June 1918; *Terre Haute Tribune,* 24 June 1918; Floy R. Painter, *That Man Debs and His Life Work* (Bloomington: Graduate Council, Indiana University, 1929), pp. 118-19; *New York Times,* 1 and 2 July 1918.

35.   *Christian Science Monitor,* 13 August 1918; *Milwaukee Leader,* 9 September 1918; *New York Times,* 9 September 1918.

36.   David A. Shannon, "Anti-War Thought and Activity of Eugene V. Debs, 1914-1921" (Master of Philosophy thesis, University of Wisconsin, 1946), pp. 33-34n.

37.   Karsner, pp. 18-19; Ginger, pp. 366-67.

38.   *Speeches of Eugene V. Debs,* pp. 23-24; Karsner, p. 21.

39.   Debs's address to the jury is included in its entirety in Karsner, pp. 23-24. Abbreviated versions may be found in the following pamphlets: *The Debs White Book; The Heritage of Debs—the Fight Against War* (Chicago: Socialist Party National Headquarters, 1935), and Scott Nearing, *The Debs Decision* (3d edition; New York: Rand School of Social Science, 1919).

40.   Karsner, pp. 46-47.

41.   An abridgment of Debs's final statement to the court is printed in *Writings and Speeches of Eugene V. Debs* (New York: Hermitage Press, 1948), pp. 437-39.

42.   Karsner, p. 55.

43.   *New York Times,* 14 and 23 September 1918; Max Eastman, "The Trial of Eugene Debs," *Liberator,* November 1918, pp. 5-12.

44.   *Toledo Times [Ohio],* 28 December 1918; *Indianapolis News,* 13 March 1919; *Duluth Truth [Minnesota],* 28 March 1919.

45.   *Debs v. United States,* 249 U.S. 211 (1919); Marshall Van Winkle, *Sixty Famous Cases* (Long Branch, N. J.: Warren S. Ayres, 1956), vol. 7, pp. 240-41.

46.   Lerner, p. 442; Ernst Freund, "The Debs Case and Freedom of Speech," *New Republic,* 3 May 1919, pp. 13 and 15; Amos Pinchot, "Debs Sent to Prison," *Appeal to Reason,* 26 April 1919; *Speeches of Eugene V. Debs,* pp. 84 and 85.

47.   Hillquit, p. 244. "The German Peace Offer," the article for which Russell was imprisoned, appeared in the 3 January 1918 issue of the *Tribunal,* a weekly newspaper issued by the No Conscription Fellowship.

48.   Zechariah Chafee, Jr., *Free Speech in the United States* (Cambridge: Harvard University Press, 1942), p. 85; Forrest R. Black, "Debs v. the United States—A Judicial Milepost on the Road to Absolutism," *University of Pennsylvania Law Review,* December 1932, pp. 174-75; Hilton, p. 223.

49.   *Atlanta Constitution,* 1 October 1919. Keller's letter to Goldman was printed in the anarchist monthly *Mother Earth Bulletin,* January 1918, p. 9; her letter to Debs appeared in both the *New York Call,* 24 April 1919, and the *Appeal to Reason,* 17 May 1919.
50.   Karsner, p. 5; *New York Call,* 18 October 1919; *Appeal to Reason,* 23 October 1920; *New York Times,* 2 February 1921.
51.   *New York Times,* 15 May 1920.
52.   Upton Sinclair, "Spirit of Debs Cannot Be Shut Up Behind Walls of Steel or Stone," *Appeal to Reason,* 26 April 1919; John Spargo, "Democracy Must Not Be Vindictive," *Independent,* 11 September 1920; George D. Herron to Woodrow Wilson, 26 September 1919, *Morris Hillquit Papers* (microfilm edition), State Historical Society of Wisconsin, 1969; Joseph P. Tumulty, *Woodrow Wilson As I Know Him* (Garden City: Doubleday, Page & Co., 1921), pp. 150–51.
53.   Van Winkle, vol. 7, p. 245.
54.   *New York Times,* 28 December 1921.
55.   Guy A. Alfred, *Convict 9653* (Glascow, n.p., n.d.), p. 9; *New York Times,* 10 July and 1 November 1923, 4 May 1925; "Soldiers' Bonus," *Omaha Free Press,* 10 October 1923.
56.   Arthur Robinson, "The Great Dreamer: An Interview with Eugene V. Debs," *Collier's,* 20 November 1926, p. 11; Victor L. Berger, *Voice and Pen of Victor L. Berger* (Milwaukee: Milwaukee Leader, 1929), p. 607.

2: MORRIS HILLQUIT, LOGICIAN OF SOCIAL REVOLUTION

1.   On 9 October 1933 the prominent Austrian Socialist Friedrich Adler responded to the news of Hillquit's death by cabling the following message to the American Socialist Party: "His clear brain, penetrating judgment, and gift of inspiring oratory always held the attention of International Socialist Congresses and made him in Europe the best known figure in the American Labour movement." (*Socialist Party of America Papers,* Perkins Library, Duke University.) Hillquit's international reputation is also noted in a *New York Times* article of the same date.
2.   The best source of information on Hillquit's early life remains his autobiography, *Loose Leaves from a Busy Life* (New York: Macmillan, 1934). The only other reasonably complete treatment of his career is Robert W. Iversen, "Morris Hillquit, American Social Democrat" (Ph.D. dissertation, State University of Iowa, 1951).
3.   William H. McLoughlin, Jr., *Billy Sunday Was His Real Name* (Chicago: University of Chicago Press, 1955), p. 282; Max Eastman, *Love and Revolution* (New York: Random House, 1964), p. 89; Leon Trotsky, *My Life* (London: Thornton Butterworth, 1930), p. 236; Joseph Freeman, *An American Testament* (New York: Farrar & Rinehart, 1936), p. 110.
4.   James Joll, *The Second International, 1889–1914* (London: Weidenfeld and Nicolson, 1955), pp. 196–98; *Socialism in Theory and Practice* (New York: Macmillan, 1909), pp. 60–61; Hillquit to W. H. Short, 12 June 1911, as printed in "Who Are the Peacemakers?" (Socialist Party leaflet, 1911), *Morris Hillquit Papers,* Tamiment Library, New York City; *Loose Leaves,* p. 145.
5.   *Omaha News,* 6 September 1914; *San Francisco Bulletin,* 17 October 1914.
6.   Typescript dated 21 September 1914, *Morris Hillquit Papers* (microfilm edition), State Historical Society of Wisconsin, 1969 (hereafter cited as *MHP*); "Socialism and War: Some Probable Effects of the War," *Metropolitan,* May 1915, p. 44; "The 'Collapse' of the International," *American Socialist,* 1 May 1915.
7.   *Revolutionary Radicalism* (Albany, N. Y.: Senate, State of New York, 1920), vol. 1, p. 1078; *New York Times,* 19 December 1914; Alexander Trachtenberg, ed., *The American Socialists and the War* (New York: Rand School of Social Science, 1917), pp. 16–19.
8.   Hillquit to Carl D. Thompson, 20 January 1915, *Socialist Party of America*

Papers, Perkins Library, Duke University; "An Unaccepted Challenge," *New York Call,* 30 January 1915.

9.   George D. Herron to Hillquit, 5 April 1915, *MHP;* Louis Fraina, "The Menace of American Militarism," *New Review,* March 1915, p. 135; "Socialism and War: III. Socialist War Tactics," *Metropolitan,* February 1915, pp. 39–41.

10.   Hillquit to Walter Lanferseik, 21 September 1914, *MHP.* Hillquit's letter of 28 December 1914 to the National Executive Committee of the American Socialist Party is printed in William E. Walling, ed., *The Socialists and the War* (New York: Henry Holt, 1915), pp. 417–19.

11.   *New York Times,* 18 July 1915; William Hard, " 'War? Never Again.' Would Socialism Do It?: An Interview with Morris Hillquit," *Everybody's,* March 1915, pp. 383–84; Augustus P. Gardner and Morris Hillquit, *Must We Arm?* (New York: Rand School of Social Science, 1915), 44 pp.; "Some current Economic and Political Problems," *Ford Hall Folks,* 21 November 1915, pp. 1–3, 8; "The War and International Socialism," *Yale Review,* October 1915, pp. 39–49.

12.   Hillquit's remarks to the Emergency Conference of Peace Forces, delivered in Chicago's Sinai Temple on February 28, appeared in the *American Socialist* of 6 March 1915 under the title "Our Duty to Europe and Ourselves." The typescript of his May 1 address to the Academy of Political and Social Science is included in the *MHP.*

13.   Gardner and Hillquit, *Must We Arm?,* pp. 28–29, 32, 34, 38, 44. Hillquit describes his visit with President Wilson in *Loose Leaves,* pp. 161–62. The full text of his remarks before the Foreign Relations Committee is available in the *American Socialist,* 1 April 1916.

14.   *Appeal to Reason,* 5 August 1916; *American Socialist,* 7 October 1916; *New York Times,* 17 October 1916. Typescripts of several of Hillquit's congressional campaign speeches are included in the *MHP.*

15.   *New York Times,* 6 and 11 February 1917. Wood denounced Hillquit at a patriotic rally in New York's Broadway Tabernacle on 13 March 1917. His remarks are quoted in part in ibid., 14 March 1917.

16.   Ibid., 5 March 1917; Louis Waldman, *Labor Lawyer* (New York: E. P. Dutton, 1944), pp. 67–68; Trotsky, pp. 235–36.

17.   *American Socialist,* 14 April 1917.

18.   Trachtenberg, pp. 3–7; David A. Shannon, *The Socialist Party of America* (New York: Macmillan, 1955), p. 102; *New York Times,* 9 May and 3 June 1917; *New York Call,* 10 May 1917; "The Socialist as Patriot," *Literary Digest,* 16 June 1917, pp. 1836–7.

19.   Lansing is quoted in *Loose Leaves,* p. 156.

20.   From a statement issued by William E. Walling, Charles E. Russell, and Ernest Poole on 8 May 1917 and quoted in the *New York Times,* 10 May 1917.

21.   Hillquit describes his work for the Peoples' Council in *Loose Leaves,* pp. 170–79.

22.   Iversen, p. 177; Irving Howe and Lewis Coser, *The American Communist Party* (Boston: Beacon Press, 1957), p. 21.

23.   *New York Times,* 15 October, 22 October and 2 November 1917; A. W. Ricker, "Victory for New York Socialists," *Pearsons's,* January 1918.

24.   *New York Times,* 24 September 1917. See the text of Hillquit's speech to the Collegiate League, 30 October 1917, *MHP.*

25.   William Hard, "The New York Mayoralty Campaign," *New Republic,* 6 October 1917, p. 270; "Mr. Hillquit Replies," ibid., 13 October 1917, p. 302; *New York Times,* 23 and 30 October 1917.

26.   *New York Times,* 2 and 3 November 1917; *New York Herald,* 2 November 1917; *New York World,* 26 October and 6 November 1917.

27.   *New York Times,* 31 October 1917; "The New York Election," *Nation,* 8 November 1917, p. 500.

28.   *Loose Leaves,* p . 193; Emma Goldman, *Living My Life* (New York: Alfred A. Knopf, 1931), vol. 2, p. 637; Lochner to Iversen, 7 May 1949, as quoted in Iversen, p. 203.

29.   The edited transcripts of Hillquit's addresses of 30 October and 4 November 1917 are in the *MHP*. See also the *New York Times*, 10 and 15 October 1917, and *Loose Leaves*, pp. 214–15.

30.   "Editorial Notes," *New Republic*, 10 November 1917, p. 31. For a similar assessment see L. [Ludwig Lore], "The New York Mayoralty Campaign," *Class Struggle*, November–December 1917, p. 101.

31.   *Loose Leaves*, pp. 217–18, 225–32, 240; *New York Times*, 18 February 1920.

32.   *Chicago Daily News*, 22 February 1918; *New York Times*, 3 March and 9 May 1918; Christopher Lasch, *The American Liberals and the Russian Revolution* (New York: Columbia University Press, 1962), p. 98; *Loose Leaves*, p. 235; Iversen, pp. 177–78; Philip S. Foner, *The Bolshevik Revolution* (New York: International Publishers, 1967), pp. 29–31.

33.   See Hillquit's address to the Fourteenth Annual Convention of the International Ladies' Garment Workers' Union in Boston, Mass., 20 May–1 June 1918, as quoted in Foner, pp. 96–97, and Hillquit's typescript "Paris and Moscow" [1919], *MHP*.

34.   For a forthright statement of Hillquit's perception of the need for such an organization see his article "What Shall Be the Foreign Policy of the United States?" *Intercollegiate Socialist*, February–March 1917, pp. 4–7.

35.   From the typescript of a manifesto prepared by Hillquit on 4 September 1919 and adopted shortly thereafter by the Socialist Party at its Emergency Convention in Chicago. *MHP*.

36.   The debate was held in Carnegie Hall on 2 February 1926. A stenographic record of the proceedings is available in *MHP*.

37.   *New York Times*, 13 May 1920.

3: MAX EASTMAN, RENAISSANCE RADICAL

1.   Milton Cantor, *Max Eastman* (New York: Twayne, 1970), Preface; Joseph Freeman, *An American Testament* (New York: Farrar and Rinehart, 1936), p. 103. Not all of Eastman's radical acquaintances thought highly of him. Emma Goldman, for example, complained that he had a poor grasp of "the true meaning of freedom" and cared little "about its actual application in life." (*Living My Life* [New York: Alfred A. Knopf, 1931], vol. 2, p. 572.) And Hutchins Hapgood not only charged that Eastman lacked "genuine democratic impulse," but lamented the latter's "overpowering ego." (*A Victorian in the Modern World* [New York: Harcourt, Brace and Co., 1939], pp. 312–13.)

2.   Eastman, *Love and Revolution* (New York: Random House, 1964), pp. 13–14.

3.   Daniel Aaron, *Writers on the Left* (New York: Harcourt, Brace and World, 1961), p. 18; Dos Passos as quoted in *Love and Revolution*, p. 17; Mabel Dodge Luhan, *Movers and Shakers* (New York, Harcourt, Brace and Co., 1936), p. 199; Irving Howe in his introduction to William O'Neill, ed., *Echoes of Revolt* (Chicago: Quadrangle Books, 1966), p. 5.

4.   "Editorials," *Liberator*, March 1918; Mencken as quoted in *Love and Revolution*, p. 195.

5.   *Since Lenin Died* (New York: Boni & Liveright, 1925), p. 12. Eastman translated four of Trotsky's books: *The Real Situation in Russia* (New York: Harcourt, Brace and Co., 1928), *The History of the Russian Revolution* (3 vols.; New York: Simon & Schuster, 1932), *The Revolution Betrayed* (Garden City: Doubleday, Doran & Co., 1937), and *The Young Lenin* (Garden City: Doubleday & Co., 1972).

6.   On Eastman's critique of Marxism as a philosophical system, see John P. Diggins, "Getting Hegel out of History: Max Eastman's Quarrel with Marxism," *American Historical Review*, February 1974, pp. 38–71.

7.   *Love and Revolution*, p. 29.

8.   *Understanding Germany* (New York: Mitchell Kennerly, 1916), pp. 2, 111, 138–43; "In Case of War," *Masses*, April 1917; Eastman letter to the *New York Call*, 30 May 1912. A staunch admirer of the I. W. W.'s activism, Eastman objected strongly to that section of the Socialist Party's constitution which called for the expulsion

of any member advocating violence, crime, or sabotage. In his opinion, the I. W. W. was "the only genuinely proletarian organization that ever existed in America." ("Abrakadabra," *Masses,* August 1913.)

9.   *Enjoyment of Living* (New York: Harper & Bros., 1948), p. 529; "War Psychology and International Socialism," *Masses,* August 1916; *Understanding Germany,* pp. 27, 85, 159; "The Religion of Patriotism," *Masses,* July 1917.

10.   "The Only Way to End War," *Masses,* December 1915; "Not Utopian," ibid., December 1914; "What Shall We Do with Patriotism?," *Survey,* 1 January 1916, p. 404.

11.   *Enjoyment of Living,* p. 529; "War Psychology and International Socialism," *Masses,* August 1916; "Editorials," *Liberator,* May 1919.

12.   "Editorials," *Masses,* March 1916; "War for War's Sake," ibid., September 1914; "Let the War Go On," ibid., October 1914.

13.   *Enjoyment of Living,* p. 533; "The Uninteresting War," *Masses,* September 1915; *Love and Revolution,* p. 26.

14.   *Enjoyment of Living,* p. 580; John Reed, "At the Throat of the Republic," *Masses,* July 1916; *Love and Revolution,* p. 25; *Understanding Germany,* p. 101.

15.   Crystal Eastman, "War and Peace," *Survey,* 30 December 1916, p. 363; *Love and Revolution,* pp. 26–30; *New York Times,* 14 January 1917; Randolph S. Bourne, *War and the Intellectuals,* edited by Carl Resek (New York: Harper & Row, 1964), p. 38n. For a full account of the American Union Against Militarism, see Blanche W. Cooke, "Woodrow Wilson and the Anti-Militarists, 1914–1918" (Ph.D. dissertation, John Hopkins University, 1970).

16.   *Love and Revolution,* pp. 28–29; O'Neill, ed., *Echoes of Revolt,* p. 22; "Advertising Democracy," *Masses,* June 1917; "Conscription for What?," ibid., July 1917.

17.   *Love and Revolution,* pp. 49, 56.

18.   Ibid., pp. 58–64; Thomas A. Maik, "A History of the *Masses* Magazine" (Ph.D. dissertation, Bowling Green State University, 1968), pp. 206–11; George P. West, "A Talk with Mr. Burleson," *International Socialist Review,* November–December 1917, p. 284; *New York Call,* 14 August 1917. As he informed the United States Senate at the end of August, Burleson regarded the *Masses* as "a leader in propaganda to discourage enlistments, prevent subscriptions to Liberty Loans, and obstruct the draft." His specific charge against the magazine's August issue was that it included four antiwar cartoons and a poem favoring the anarchists Emma Goldman and Alexander Berkman, who were convicted in July of conspiracy to obstruct the operation of the selective service law. (*Congressional Record,* 65th Congress, 1st Session, p. 6852).

19.   Both Eastman's Letter (which includes words of praise for the peace conditions declared by the President on 24 August 1917) and Wilson's reply were printed on the front page of the *New York Times* of 28 September 1917.

20.   "The *Masses* Staff Under Arrest," *Survey,* 24 November 1917, p. 207.

21.   Dell as quoted in Louis Untermeyer, *From Another World* (New York: Harcourt, Brace and Co., 1939), p. 68; *Love and Revolution,* p. 85; Maik, pp. 223–30; Josephine Bell, "A Tribute," *Masses,* August 1917.

22.   *New York Times,* 23 April 1918; "Editorials," *Liberator,* March 1918; Floyd Dell, "The Story of the Trial," ibid., June 1918.

23.   *Max Eastman's Address to the Jury in the Second Masses Trial* (New York: The Liberator Publishing Co., 1919), pp. 3, 17–18, 46; *New York Times,* 11 January 1919; *Love and Revolution,* p. 85; John Reed, "About the second *Masses* Trial," *Liberator,* December 1918; Floyd Dell, *Homecoming* (New York: Farrar & Rinehart, 1933), p. 316; Art Young, *Art Young* (New York: Sheridan House, 1939), p. 351.

24.   *Love and Revolution,* pp. 123 and xi–xii.

4: JOHN REED, REVOLUTIONARY JOURNALIST

1.   Richard O'Connor and Dale L. Walker, *The Lost Revolutionary* (New York: Harcourt, Brace and World, 1967), p. 37; Jerry A. Vavra, "By the Kremlin Wall," *American Mercury,* January 1956, pp. 100–01; Max Lerner, "John Reed: No Legend," *Nation,* 29 April 1936, p. 552.

2.   Walter Lippmann, "Legendary John Reed," *New Republic,* 26 December 1914, p. 15; "The Traders' War," *Masses,* September 1914. According to Theodore Draper, the war "gave Reed his first profound, personal political cause." (*The Roots of American Communism* [New York: Viking Press, 1957], p. 118.) Draper's judgment is confirmed by H. V. Kaltenborn, a Harvard classmate of Reed who later became a noted radio commentator: "When he [Reed] later visited me after his first experience at the front I recognized a profound intellectual change. He had become much more mature and much more radical. He hated everything about the war and resented a governmental system that made war possible." (*Fifty Fabulous Years, 1900-1950*) [New York: G. P. Putnam's Sons, 1950], p. 43).

3.   "The Traders' War," *Masses,* September 1914; "Rule Britannia!" (unpublished typescript of Autumn 1914), *John Reed Papers,* Houghton Library, Harvard University (Hereafter cited as *JRP*). Reed's critical attitude toward the British, in particular the British aristocracy, is also expressed in two other articles: "Shot at Sunrise" (unpublished typescript of 22 September 1914), ibid., and "The Englishman," *Metropolitan,* October 1914, pp. 39–40.

4.   As quoted in Bertam D. Wolfe, "The Harvard Man in the Kremlin Wall," *American Heritage,* February 1960, p. 99.

5.   "With the Allies," *Metropolitan,* December 1914, p. 15; "Rule Britannia!," *JRP;* "The Worst Thing in Europe," *Masses,* March 1915.

6.   Julian Street, "A Soviet Saint: The Story of John Reed," *Saturday Evening Post,* 13 September 1930, p. 8. On Reed's experiences at the German military hospital see his article "In the German Trenches," *Metropolitan,* April 1915, pp. 7–8.

7.   Dunn, who was with Reed in the German trench—and had also "fired twice" at the French lines—described the incident in the *New York Post* of 27 February 1915.

8.   *The War in Eastern Europe* (New York: Charles Scribner's Sons, 1916), p. 5; "The Most Tragic Incident I Saw in the War," *New York World,* 22 April 1917; *New York Call,* 7 January 1916; *New York Telegraph,* 10 March 1916; *Brooklyn Daily Eagle,* 18 February 1916.

9.   On the termination of Reed's relationship with the *Metropolitan* see O'Connor, pp. 187–88, and Granville Hicks, *John Reed* (New York: Macmillan, 1936), pp. 228–29.

10.   *New York Times,* 28 October and 3 November 1916; letter from Reed to the National Executive Commmtte, 13 October 1916, *Socialist Party of America Papers,* Perkins Library, Duke University.

11.   O'Connor, p. 188; "Whose War?" *Masses,* April 1917 (Reprinted in the *New York Call,* 18 March 1917).

12.   Hicks, pp. 233–35; *New York Times,* 13 April 1917.

13.   "Almost Thirty," *JRP.* The essay was posthumously published in the *New Republic,* 15 and 29 April 1936, pp. 267–70, 332–36.

14.   On 3 July 1917 Reed appeared as a character witness at the two anarchists' trial. (*New York Times,* 4 July 1917.) He subsequently referred to their conviction and to the "wholesale suppression of the radical press" as proof that in America "there are no Constitutional safeguards worth the powder to blow them to hell." ("One Solid Month of Liberty," *Masses,* September 1917).

15.   "Wealth, Beauty, War—Skylark," *New York Mail,* 7 June 1917; "Macdougal

Alley Trips Gayly to the Relief of War Horrors," ibid., 13 June 1917.

16.   "This Unpopular War," *Seven Arts,* August 1917; "Across the War World" (unpublished typescript of August 1917), *JRP;* Street, "A Soviet Saint," pp. 8-9. 65, 67-68; Vintage Russian Library edition of Reed's *Ten Days That Shook the World* (New York: Random House, 1960).

17.   Reed appeared at the Federal Building as ordered and was arraigned before Judge Rufus E. Foster who fixed his bail at $2,000 (*New York Times,* 30 April 1918).

18.   Benjamin Gitlow, *The Whole of Their Lives* (New York: Charles Scribner's Sons, 1948), p. 22; "The Social Revolution in Court," *Liberator,* September 1918; *New York Times,* 4 October 1918; Hicks, pp. 316-19.

19.   John P. Diggins, *The American Left in the Twentieth Century* (New York: Harcourt Brace Jovanovich, 1973), pp. 97 and 105; George F. Kennan, *Soviet-American Relations, 1917-1920.* vol. 1: *Russia Leaves the War* (Princeton: Princeton University Press, 1956), p. 69.

5: EMMA GOLDMAN, ANARCHIST PACIFIST

1.   David Karsner, *Talks with Debs in Terre Haute (and Letters from Lindlahr)* (New York: The New York Call, 1922), p. 69; *Nation,* June 1922, p. 739; Hoover as quoted in Richard Drinnon, *Rebel in Paradise* (Chicago: University of Chicago Press, 1961), p. 215; Philip S. Foner, *History of the Labor Movement in the United States.* vol. 4: *The Industrial Workers of the World, 1905-1917* (New York: International Publishers, 1965), p. 201.

2.   Daniel Aaron, *Writers on the Left* (New York: Harcourt, Brace & World, 1961), p. 32.

3.   *My Disillusionment in Russia* (London: C. W. Daniel, 1925), p. 252.

4.   *Emma Goldman Papers,* New York Public Library (hereafter cited as *EGP*).

5.   "What I Believe," *New York World,* 19 July 1908; "Was My Life Worth Living?," *Harper's,* December 1934, p. 53.

6.   Frank Harris, *Contemporary Portraits,* Fourth Series (New York: Brentano's, 1923), pp. 227-28. On Goldman's opposition to the Spanish-American and Boer wars see her autobiography, *Living My Life* (New York: Alfred A. Knopf, 1931), vol. 1, pp. 226-27, 255-57.

7.   *Living My Life,* vol. 1, p. 428; "Patriotism: A Menace to Liberty," in *Anarchism and Other Essays* (New York: Mother Earth Publishing Assoc., 1911), pp. 134, 138-39, 149-50; *EGP,* untitled and undated typescript file on children.

8.   *New York Evening Post,* 30 June 1908; "Patriotism: A Menace to Liberty," *Anarchism,* p. 145.

9.   *Mother Earth,* January 1915, p. 343; ibid., December, 1914, pp. 320-24; ibid., February 1915, pp. 362-68. See also the editorial "Some Emma Goldman Lectures in Chicago," *The Little Review,* October 1914, p. 36.

10.   *Mother Earth,* May 1915, p. 119; ibid., March 1917, p. 6.

11.   *Living My Life,* vol. 2, p. 565; *Mother Earth,* December 1915, pp. 333, 335-36, 338; ibid., March 1917, pp. 10-11.

12.   *Living My Life,* vol. 2, p. 598; *Mother Earth,* June 1917, p. 113.

13.   *New York Tribune,* 19 May 1917; *Living My Life,* vol. 2, p. 606; *New York Herald,* 5 June 1917.

14.   Unidentified newspaper clipping of 12 June 1917 in the Emma Goldman scrapbook compiled by Agnes Inglis and housed in the Labadie Collection at the University of Michigan; *New York Times,* 12 June 1917.

15.   *New York Times,* 15 June 1917; *Living My Life,* vol. 2, p. 609; *Mother Earth,* June 1917, p. 97.

16.   *Mother Earth,* June 1917, pp. 101-02.

17.   *EGP.*

18.   *New York Times,* 17 June 1917. On the trial see ibid., 28 June to 8 July 1917;

Living My Life, vol. 2, pp. 614–23; "The Trial and Conviction of Emma Goldman and Alexander Berkman," *Mother Earth,* July 1917, pp. 129–37.

19.   Prosecutor Content's summation is available in *Anarchism on Trial* (New York: Mother Earth Publishing Assoc., n.d.), pp. 67–72. Goldman's address to the jury was printed in its entirety in *Mother Earth,* July 1917, pp. 150–61.

20.   *Living My Life,* vol. 2, pp. 622–23.

21.   Ibid., p. 620.

22.   *Selective Draft Law Cases,* 245 U. S. 366 (1918); *Goldman et al. v. United States,* 245 U. S. 474 (1918).

23.   In "What I Believe," published in the *New York World* of 19 July 1908, Goldman complained of the impression that the public had of her and her beliefs: "Such blood-curdling and incoherent stories have been circulated about me, it is no wonder that the average human being has palpitation of the heart at the very mention of the name Emma Goldman. It is too bad we no longer live in the times when witches were burned at the stake or tortured to drive the evil spirit out of them. For, indeed, Emma Goldman is a witch! True, she does not eat little children, but she does many worse things. She manufactures bombs and gambles in crowned heads. B-r-r-r!"

6: WILLIAM D. HAYWOOD, PROLETARIAN ACTIVIST

1.   Harvey Goldberg, ed., *American Radicals* (New York: Monthly Review Press, 1957), p. 179.

2.   Max Eastman, *Enjoyment of Living* (New York: Harper & Bros., 1948), p. 448; "Editorial Paragraphs" [unsigned obituary on Haywood], *Nation,* 30 May 1928, p. 601.

3.   *World's Work,* 1913, p. 417. Joseph R. Conlin points out in his excellent biography of Haywood that the latter's attitude toward violence altered following his career with the Western Federation of Miners: "Fresh from the mines, Haywood had been easy with talk of dynamite and violence as possible means to the miners' ends," but "he seemed to realize it was at best an unproductive tool as early as 1900. . . . His near-scrape with execution in Idaho confirmed him in this policy. . . . (*Big Bill Haywood and the Radical Union Movement* [Syracuse, New York: Syracuse University Press, 1969], p. 115.)

4.   Hutchins Hapgood, *A Victorian in the Modern World* (New York: Harcourt, Brace and Co., 1939), pp. 293–94; *New York Times,* 2 and 7 February 1914.

5.   *New York Times,* 20 April 1914; William D. Haywood, "Jaurès and the General Strike Against War," *International Socialist Review,* September 1914, pp. 145–46.

6.   *Bill Haywood's Book* (New York: International Publishers, 1929), pp. 280–81, 287; *Solidarity,* 31 October 1914; Joyce L. Kornbluh, *Rebel Voices* (Ann Arbor: University of Michigan Press, 1964), p. 316; letter, dated 9 February 1917, in the pardon file of Richard Brazier, No. 15/132, Department of Justice Records, National Archives, Washington, D. C.

7.   *Christian Science Monitor,* 31 July 1918; "Everlasting Peace," *International Socialist Review,* April 1915, p. 588; Melvyn Dubofsky, "The Radicalism of the Dispossessed: William Haywood and the IWW," in *Dissent,* edited by Alfred F. Young (DeKalb: Northern Illinois University Press, 1968), p. 202.

8.   John N. Beffel, "Four Radicals," *American Mercury,* April 1932, p. 442; Patrick Renshaw, *The Wobblies* (Garden City: Doubleday & Co., 1967), p. 217. Indicative of his low opinion of Gompers, Haywood once described the A. F. L. president as "a squat specimen of humanity" with "small snapping eyes, a hard cruel mouth," and "a personality vain, conceited, petulant and vindictive." (Bernard A. Weisberger, "Here Come the Wobblies!," *American Heritage,* June 1967, p. 32.)

9.   Conlin, pp. 183–84; Lowell S. Hawley and Ralph B. Potts, *Counsel for the Damned* (Philadelphia and New York: J. B. Lippincott, 1953), pp. 225–26; Philip Taft, "The Federal Trials of the I. W. W.," *Labor History,* Winter, 1962, p. 66.

10. William Preston, Jr., *Aliens and Dissenters* (Cambridge: Harvard University Press, 1963), p. 90; Kornbluh, p. 318.

11. Ralph Chaplin, *Wobbly* (Chicago: University of Chicago Press, 1948), p. 206; *Solidarity*, 24 March 1917. "Christians at War" is reprinted in Kornbluh, p. 328.

12. See, for example, "Kaiser's Coin Pays for I. W. W. Sabotage," *San Francisco Chronicle*, 22 February 1918, and "I. W. W. Funds Traced to German Sources," *Anaconda Standard* (Butte, Montana), 25 February 1918.

13. *Congressional Record*, 65th Congress, 1st Session, p. 6104. Two other hostile versions of the meaning of "I. W. W." were widely circulated beginning in the summer of 1917: "I Won't Work" and "I Want Whiskey." *Solidarity* countered with its own version: "I Will Win" (4 August 1917).

14. *Evening Capital News* (Boise, Idaho), 7 July 1917.

15. *Bill Haywood's Book*, p. 299. Conlin points out (p. 181) that "The largest proportion of foreign born in any mass arrest of IWW members was about 50 per cent, and the union's leaders were native Americans almost to the man."

16. "What Haywood Says of the I. W. W.," *Survey*, 11 August 1917, pp. 429–30. See also the *New York Times*, 13 July 1917.

17. Victor S. Yarros, "The Story of the I. W. W. Trial," *Survey*, 7 September 1918, p. 630.

18. Carl Sandburg, "Haywood Longs for 'Other Boys' in Jail," *International Socialist Review*, November–December 1917, pp. 277–78; "I. W. W. Raid Regarded First Attack in Campaign to Jail All Class Conscious Workers," *Michigan Socialist*, 5 October 1917; Louis C. Fraina, "The I. W. W. Trial," *Class Struggle*, November–December 1917, p. 1.

19. Helen Keller, "In Behalf of the I. W. W.," *Liberator*, March 1918; Chaplin, p. 224; Bruère in the *New York Evening Post*, 14 November 1917; John Reed, "The Social Revolution in Court," *Liberator*, September 1918; *Chicago Daily Tribune*, 19 August 1918.

20. Melvyn Dubofsky, *We Shall Be All* (Chicago: Quadrangle Books, 1969), pp. 434 and 436; Hawley and Potts, p. 128; *Christian Science Monitor*, 3 July 1918.

21. Haywood's testimony is available in the 312-page pamphlet *Evidence and Cross Examination of William D. Haywood in the Case of the U. S. A. v. Wm. D. Haywood et al.* (Chicago: Industrial Workers of the World, 1918).

22. Nebeker alleged that at least nine members had been expelled from the union for enlisting in the United States Army or in the service of one of her allies. (*Christian Science Monitor*, 23 May 1918.)

23. Richard Brazier, "The Mass I. W. W. Trial of 1918: A Retrospect," *Labor History*, Spring 1966, p. 188.

24. *Survey*, 7 September 1918; Beffel, p. 444; *New York Times*, 11 October 1920. See also *Haywood et al. v. United States*, 268 Fed. 795 (7th Circuit, 1920).

25. "Branding the I. W. W.," *Literary Digest*, 31 August 1918, p. 14; "To the President," *New Republic*, 19 April 1919, pp. 383–84.

26. *World's Work*, October 1918, pp. 581–82.

27. Emma Goldman, *Living My Life* (New York: Alfred A. Knopf, 1931), vol. 2, p. 904.

BIBLIOGRAPHY

SELECTED AND ANNOTATED

A list of all the manuscript collections, public documents, books, pamphlets, reports, dissertations, newspapers, and journal articles consulted in preparing this study would not only be of excessive length, but would duplicate unnecessarily the reference notes on pages 136-146. The bibliography is therefore limited to the most important sources relevant to the work's central theme: the antiwar thought and activities of the "six who protested" and what happened to these nonconformists as a result.

MANUSCRIPTS

Emma Goldman Papers at the New York Public Library. The collection is important for her correspondence with American radicals and liberals and for many of her early lectures.

Eugene V. Debs Collection at New York's Tamiment Library (formerly the Rand School of Social Science). The materials most useful to this study are clippings contained in the *Eugene Debs Scrapbook*, especially volumes nine and ten, which cover the years 1910-1920. Unfortunately, soon after Debs's death in 1926, his widow destroyed most of his letters. The scattered letters that survive—in this and other collections—shed little light upon his opposition to war.

John Reed Papers at Harvard University's Houghton Library. The collection consists of twenty-nine boxes and includes many of Reed's letters and unpublished manuscripts as well as miscellaneous newspaper clippings and articles from periodicals.

Joseph A. Labadie Collection in the library of the University of Michigan. For a collection noted for its I. W. W. materials, the Labadie is disappointingly meager for William D. Haywood. Nonetheless, it contains many scattered items impossible to find elsewhere. A scrapbook compiled by the late Agnes Inglis deserves special mention: *The Great Chicago I. W. W. Trial of 1918.*

Morris Hillquit Papers in the library of the Wisconsin State Historical Society at Madison. The microfilm edition of these papers was used (10 reels accompanied by a pamphlet guide). The collection includes copies of Hillquit's speeches and debates, his correspondence, and newspaper clippings documenting almost every phase of his wartime activities. It is without question the most fruitful of the manuscript sources consulted in writing this book.

Socialist Party of America Papers in Duke University's Perkins Library. Since 1975 these papers have been available for purchase from the Microfilm Corporation of America (over 140 reels accompanied by a printed index and guide). Although the collection is of limited value as regards the specific concerns of the present work, its overall importance to researchers interested in American Socialism, labor, and the left is immense. The basic manuscript collection for the Socialist Party, it contains official correspondence, memoranda, membership and financial records, pamphlets, stenographic records of meetings, and press releases.

BOOKS, PAMPHLETS, DISSERTATIONS

Aaron, Daniel. *Writers on the Left: Episodes in American Literary Communism.* (New York: Harcourt, Brace & World, 1961.) The best commentary on the radical literary scene, with ample coverage given to Eastman and his days on the *Masses* and the *Liberator*.

Bindler, Norman. "American Socialism and the First World War." (Ph.D. dissertation, New York University, 1970.) A detailed examination of the motives, ideology, and influences which determined the Socialist Party's antiwar stand. Somewhat less attention is paid public and governmental reaction to that stand.

Brissenden, Paul F. *The I. W. W.: A Study of American Syndicalism.* (New York: Columbia University Press, 1919.) The classic history of the I. W. W. Concerned largely with that organization's internal, institutional development.

Cantor, Milton. *Max Eastman.* (New York: Twayne, 1970.) A brief interpretive biography by a highly respected authority on American radicalism and the labor movement.

Chafee, Zechariah, Jr. *Free Speech in the United States.* (Cambridge: Harvard University Press, 1941.) The best summary of cases involving Socialists between 1917 and 1937. The author, for many years a member of the faculty of the Harvard Law School, was an active defender of the Socialists during the so-called Red Scare.

Chaplin, Ralph. *Wobbly: The Rough-and-Tumble Story of an American Radical.* (Chicago: University of Chicago Press, 1948.) The reminiscences of a former I. W. W. editor and poet who later found salvation in Christianity and anti-communism. An essential source of information on Haywood's personal life.

Conlin, Joseph R. *Big Bill Haywood and the Radical Union Movement.* (Syracuse: Syracuse University Press, 1969.) The only full-length biography of Haywood. Highly sympathetic,but thoroughly researched and extremely well written. As would be true of any biography of Haywood, the work suffers from the fact that there are no "Haywood Papers." Students of the Wobbly leader's life and career must content themselves with the limited material (none of it especially valuable as regards his opposition to the war) provided in such manuscript sources as the Labadie Collection of the University of Michigan Library; the I. W. W. Collection in the Labor History Archives of Wayne State University; the Socialist Party of America Collection in the Duke University Library; and the Tamiment Library of New York City.

Curti, Merle E. *Peace or War: The American Struggle, 1636–1936.* (New York: W. W. Norton, 1936.) For many years the primary scholarly survey of the American peace movement.

Dell, Floyd. *Homecoming: An Autobiography.* (New York: Farrar & Rinehart, 1933.) By one of the defendants in the two *Masses* trials.

Dowell, Eldridge F. *A History of Criminal Syndicalism Legislation in the United States.* (Baltimore: John Hopkins Press, 1939.) A description and analysis of the laws inspired by the anarchist doctrine of violence.

Draper, Theodore. *The Roots of American Communism.* (New York: Viking Press, 1957.) Essential reading for anyone interested in the immediate postwar origins of the Communist Party and Communist Labor Party. Extremely useful as background, since it gives a detailed account of Socialist Party struggles and of the schismatic character of American radicalism.

Drinnon, Richard. *Rebel in Paradise: A Biography of Emma Goldman.* (Chicago: University of Chicago Press, 1961.) Widely recognized as the best treatment of Goldman's life.

Dubofsky, Melvyn. *We Shall Be All: A History of the Industrial Workers of the World.* (Chicago: Quadrangle Books, 1969.) An exhaustive study by a foremost authority on American labor history. Indispensable for students of the I. W. W.

Eastman, Max. *Enjoyment of Living.* (New York: Harper & Brothers, 1948.) The first of Eastman's two volumes of autobiography.

———. *Love and Revolution: My Journey Through an Epoch.* (New York: Random House, 1964.) Concluding volume of Eastman's autobiography. The contents of the Max Eastman archives, housed in Indiana University's Lilly Library, make his autobiography of particular significance to those interested in his antiwar activities. The archives contain very little on the WWI period, since Eastman was traveling a lot in those days and simply did not save files or correspondence.

———. *Understanding Germany: The Only Way to End the War and Other Essays.* (New York: Mitchell Kennerley, 1916.) An extremely important source of Eastman's early reactions to the war.

Egbert, Donald Drew, and Stow Persons, eds. *Socialism and American Life.* 2 vols. (Princeton: Princeton University Press, 1952.) The first volume is notable for Daniel Bell's lengthy essay, "The Background and Development of Marxian Socialism in the United States," which traces the development—since the late nineteenth century—of all the Marxian political parties and a few other radical political movements as well. The second volume constitutes the most wide-ranging bibliography on Socialism in this country yet published.

Evidence and Cross Examination of William D. Haywood in the Case of the U. S. A. v. Wm. D. Haywood, et al. (Chicago: Industrial Workers of the World, 1918.) This lengthy pamphlet (312 pages) is basic to understanding Haywood's role in the 1918 Chicago trial of Wobblies charged with conspiring to obstruct the Selective Service Act and to violate the Espionage Act.

Fine, Nathan. *Labor and Farmer Parties in the United States, 1828-1928.* (New York: Russell & Russell, 1961.) An invaluable source of information on the Socialist Labor Party and the Socialist Party. First published in 1928 by the Rand School of Social Science.

Foner, Philip S. *History of the Labor Movement in the United States.* vol. 4: *The Industrial Workers of the World, 1905-1917.* (New York: International Publishers, 1965.) A detailed and basically accurate work which has become a major information source on the I. W.W.

Freeman, Joseph. *An American Testament: A Narrative of Rebels and Romantics.* (New York: Farrar & Rinehart, 1936.) Reminiscences by a leading American Communist later expelled from the party. Freeman knew Eastman and comments extensively on the *Masses,* its contributors, viewpoints, aspirations.

Ginger, Ray. *The Bending Cross: A Biography of Eugene V. Debs.* (New Brunswick: Rutgers University Press, 1949.) Without question the best full-dress treatment of Debs's life.

Goldman, Emma. *Living My Life.* 2 vols. (New York: Alfred A. Knopf, 1931.) A highly personal and vivid account of her life as a revolutionary.

Haywood, William D. *Bill Haywood's Book.* (New York: International Publishers, 1929.) Written during the I. W. W. leader's exile in the Soviet Union and published shortly after his death. A generally disappointing work, it has been a subject of controversy ever since the American Communist Benjamin Gitlow alleged that prior to publication it was revised to conform to "the Party line" by the Comintern Publishing Department's U. S. representative, Alexander Trachtenberg. Yet, while one cannot be certain as to the precise nature of Haywood's role in writing it, the book remains the first source for the researcher on the subject.

Hicks, Granville. *John Reed: The Making of a Revolutionary.* (New York: Macmillan, 1936.) A fascinating and instructive biography of the archetypal Revolutionary hero. Also of interest for its portrayal of New York's radical community during the war years.

Hillquit, Morris. *Loose Leaves from a Busy Life.* (New York: Macmillan, 1934.) Hillquit's autobiography, published shortly after his death. Contains much useful material on the history of the Socialist Party down to the split of 1919.

Iversen, Robert W. "Morris Hillquit, American Social Democrat: A Study of the American Left from Haymarket to the New Deal." (Ph.D., dissertation, State University of Iowa, 1951.) Next to *Loose Leaves from a Busy Life,* the most valuable source of information on Hillquit's career.

Karsner, David. *Debs: His Authorized Life and Letters from Woodstock Prison to Atlanta.* (New York: Boni and Liveright, 1919.) Detailed coverage of Debs's 1918 trial.

O'Connor, Richard, and Dale L. Walker. *The Lost Revolutionary: A Biography of John Reed.* (New York: Harcourt, Brace & World, 1967.) Insightful, beautifully written. Complement's Hicks's biography.

Peterson, H. C., Gilbert C. Fite. *Opponents of War, 1917-1918.* (Madison: University of Wisconsin Press, 1957.) An outstanding treatment of the conflict between prowar and antiwar people, expahizing the victimization of the latter by super-patriots and extreme conservatives who displayed an intemperance that would have done credit to the wildest of radicals.

Preston, William, Jr. *Aliens and Dissenters: Federal Suppression of Radicals, 1903-1933.* (Cambridge: Harvard University Press, 1963.) The definitive study of the federal government's attempts to curb radicals. Considerable attention is paid the wartime campaign against the I. W. W.

Reed, John. *The War in Eastern Europe.* (New York: Charles Scribner's Sons, 1916.) Comprised of articles recounting Reed's experiences as a war correspondent for the *Metropolitan,* April–October, 1915.

Shannon, David A. *The Socialist Party of America: A History.* (New York: Macmillan, 1955.) The best single volume on the Socialist Party.

Trachtenberg, Alexander, ed. *The American Labor Year Book, 1917-18.* (New York: Rand School of Social Science, 1918.) Part of a series of volumes published annually or bi-annually during the period 1916-1932 by the Rand School's Labor Research Department. The series provides a running history of the Socialist Party as well as other radical and labor movements both in the United States and abroad.

——, ed. *The American Socialists and the War.* (New York: Rand School of Social Science, 1917.) An essential collection of documents illustrating the historical attitude of the Socialist Party toward WWI. Includes an introduction by Hillquit.

Weinstein, James. *The Decline of Socialism in America, 1912-1925.* (New York: Monthly Review Press, 1967.) Contrary to David A. Shannon and other academic historians, who have agreed that the Socialist Party started on a irreversible decline in 1912 and that it was finally destroyed during WWI, Weinstein argues that the party grew in strength and popularity during the war.

Writings and Speeches of Eugene V. Debs. Introduction by Arthur M. Schlesinger, Jr. (New York: Hermitage Press, 1948.) In many ways the best of a number of works containing selections from Debs's writings and speeches. Draws heavily from Socialist periodicals.

ARTICLES AND PERIODICALS

American Socialist. This weekly, published in Chicago, was the official organ of the Socialist Party from 1914 to 1917 and is an essential source for Debs's view of the war. It was the first periodical to run afoul of the Post Office Department. On 30 June 1917, it was held up in the mail on the claim that the June 16 issue had violated the provisions of the Espionage Act of June 15. Subsequently, its second-class mailing privileges were revoked by Postmaster General Albert S. Burleson.

Appeal to Reason. Published in Girard, Kansas, this weekly Socialist journal had its greatest circulation and influence in the Midwest. Although during the early years of the war Debs was prominently featured in its pages, the *Appeal to Reason* was largely the mouthpiece of Allan L. Benson, the Socialist Party's candidate for the presidency in 1916. Dubbed "The Squeal of Treason" after the United States entered the war in 1917, the journal soon bowed before governmental pressure and toned down its opposition to the conflict.

Black, Forrest R. "Debs v. the United States—A Judicial Milepost on the Road to Absolutism," *University of Pennsylvania Law Review*, 81, 2 (December 1932), 160-75. A noted legal scholar's spirited criticism of the disposition of the Debs case. Argues that Debs's guilt was not proven.

Brazier, Richard. "The Mass I. W. W. Trial of 1918: A Retrospect," *Labor History*, 7, 2 (Spring 1966), 178-92. Brazier, a Wobbly into the 1960s, was among those convicted in the 1918 trial. He sat in prison while Haywood fled to Russia.

Carroll, Thomas F. "Freedom of Speech and of the Press in War Time: The Espionage Act," *Michigan Law Review*, 17, 8 (June 1919), 621-65. A useful overview complementing the large number of articles on specific cases.

Class Struggle. A left-wing Socialist periodical published in New York from 1917 until the founding of the Communist and Communist Labor parties in 1919.

Dubofsky, Melvyn. "The Radicalism of the Dispossessed: William Haywood and the IWW." In *Dissent: Explorations in the History of American Radicalism,* edited by Alfred F. Young (De Kalb, Illinois: Northern Illinois University Press, 1968), pp. 175-213. Perhaps the best short treatment of the I. W. W. written to date.

Intercollegiate Socialist. A New York monthly established by the Intercollegiate Socialist Society in 1913 to promote Socialism among college men and women. A special supplement of April-May 1917 was devoted to a symposium on "Socialists and the Problems of War." The magazine was subsequently renamed *Socialist Review* (1919-1921) and then *Labor Age* (1921-1933).

International Socialist Review. This important Socialist monthly was published in Chicago by Charles H. Kerr from 1900 to 1918. Beginning as a serious scholarly journal devoted mainly to familiarizing the American worker with European Socialist thought, by 1912 the *Review* had become a militant organ which championed the I. W. W. and the so-called "red" wing of the Socialist Party. It opened its pages to Eugene Debs's more controversial pronouncements, added Wobbly leader William D. Haywood to its list of contributing editors, and—in January 1916—even printed excerpts from the pamphlet *Socialism and War* by the Russian Bolsheviks Vladimir Lenin and Gregory Zinoviev. During the war, it shared the fate of the *American Socialist* and other radical periodicals, dying a death of government attrition.

Masses. Published in New York, this monthly magazine was founded by Piet Vlag in 1911 and was later transformed by Max Eastman from a rather mild organ of moderate Socialism into "the Bible of the radical avante-garde." A major source of the antiwar writings of both Eastman and John Reed, it was suppressed by the government in 1917. Its successor, the *Liberator* (1918-1924), reflected the early American Communist movement emerging in 1919.

Metropolitan. During the early stages of the war in Europe, this New York-based magazine was essentially an organ of Socialist reform and, as such, included pointedly antiwar articles by both Morris Hillquit and John Reed. Beginning in early 1915, however, the magazine moved steadily away from a Socialist position and toward a pro-Allied stance.

Mother Earth. An anarchist monthly published in New York by Emma Goldman and Alexander Berkman from 1906 to August 1917, when the postal authorities barred it from the mails. *Mother Earth Bulletin,* its successor (described by Goldman as "the wee Babe of Mother Earth . . . born into a tragic, disintegrating world"), began publication in October 1917, but the following May it, too, was declared unmailable.

National Rip-Saw. Published in St. Louis, Missouri, beginning August 1914, this Socialist organ featured an editorial column by Eugene Debs. Harrassed by Postmaster General Albert S. Burleson, and hoping to dodge the prohibitions of the Espionage Act and continue a free editorial policy, it changed its name to *Social Revolution* in March 1917. The last issue appeared in May 1918.

New York Call. A leading Socialist daily published by the followers of Morris Hillquit from 1908 to 1923. It analyzed the war on a day-to-day basis in fine detail—and in such critical fashion that it had to pay full first-class postage after 13 November 1917.

New York Times. Consulted on every aspect of this study. An indispensable source.

Reed, John. "Almost Thirty," *New Republic,* 86 (15 April 1936), 267-70; (29 April 1936), 332-36. Reed penned this fascinating autobiographical essay during the summer of 1917, at a time when he was despondent and plagued by self-doubt. His career had reached a low point; the antiwar movement seemed a failure; and the class struggle was moribund.

Taft, Philip. "The Federal Trials of the IWW," *Labor History,* 3, 1 (Winter 1962), 57-91. A scholarly reassessment by a past president of the Industrial Relations Research Association and of the Labor Historians Association.

INDEX

155

DATE DUE

1-16-79			
GAYLORD			PRINTED IN U.S.A